Mike Stannett   S~

*S/red*
*3 · ∞*

# Modular
# Software Design

△ Chartwell-Bratt                    △ Studentlitteratur

**British Library Cataloguing in Publication Data**
Stannett, Mike
    Modular software design
    1. Computer systems. Software. Development
    I. Title II. Dickinson, Sean
    005.1

ISBN 0-86238-266-1

© Mike Stannett, Sean Dickinson and Chartwell-Bratt Ltd, 1990

Chartwell-Bratt (Publishing and Training) Ltd
ISBN 0-86238-266-1

Printed in Sweden,
Studentlitteratur, Lund
ISBN 91-44-33351-X

1  2  3  4  5  6  7  8  9  10 | 1994  93  92  91  90

# Contents

## Chapter 5: Structure and Style

## Chapter 6: Testing

## Appendix A: A Typical Project

## Bibliography

# Chapter 1

# Overview

---

The objective of this course is to give you
alternative views of the software development process,
illustrating how modular software can be developed
using a number of tried and tested formal and semi-
formal techniques. By the end of the course you should
be able to apply established software principles in a
variety of development environments.

---

## Quality

Perhaps the most important objective of this course is to teach you
something about design *quality*. Anyone can write a small *ad hoc* piece of
software, after just a few programming lessons - and sometimes it might
even work properly. Unfortunately, as any beginner will tell you, it's very
easy to make mistakes. Increasingly, however, software is being relied upon
to take charge of all sorts of complicated control systems, ranging from fly-
by-wire aircraft to steel production, telecommunications to supermarket
check-outs. Mistakes can be expensive and, in extreme cases, can kill.
Clearly, we need to ensure that the likelihood of errors occurring in our
software is reduced to a minimum.

One way to reduce the risk of errors is to make the systems we
design easier for other people to understand. It's a useful rule-of-thumb in

education that the extent to which someone understands something is reflected in their ability to explain it to others. If you can't explain it easily in simple terms, then you probably don't understand it yourself - and if you don't understand what you're doing, you probably shouldn't be doing it. This is especially true in software engineering, where the simplest mistakes can have such major consequences.

But there's another reason why you should make your designs easy to follow. The software industry is increasingly fluid, and you are likely to move between companies many times during your career (very frequently, if you become a consultant). This means that, if you are working as a member of a team developing a large software product, you may well leave before its completion. You owe it to your successors to leave clear explanations of your work so far (remember that *you* may be someone's successor at your new company).

Moreover, software systems are now so large that no individual can design them alone. For example, more work goes into developing a large operating system than was involved in the development of nuclear weapons technology. Such large systems can only be designed by teams of people working together. But teams have to communicate. There's no point designing a system that runs perfectly on your PC, if your team mate's system is incompatible with your own. Clear and complete explanations of what you're doing (and why) are essential if you're not going to encounter major problems later.

**Modularity**

One way to reduce the problems inherent in designing large software systems is to adopt a *modular* approach. There are many different definitions of modularity; here is our first. Modules are independent, distinct functional components - building blocks from which the system is constructed. Large systems, as we shall discuss later, will be designed by one or more teams working in collaboration; the obvious thing to do is to make this collaborative approach to software design as effective as possible. What does this mean in practice?

Consider the design of a fairly simple system - a data retrieval system. If you think about it, there are two fairly obvious parts to this system. Since you need to deal with data, you will presumably need to develop some form of data base, together with the functions you'll require to manipulate it efficiently. But this isn't enough. You also need to ensure that the system is usable - and this involves the development of an appropriate user interface. So we can split the system into two parts[1] (*Figure 1.1*).

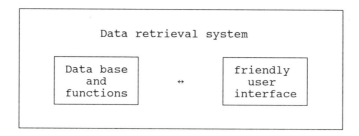

Figure 1.1

These two parts are not particularly related to each other, and could be developed by two different teams. Of course, they would have to agree on *some* features - like which functions the user should have available - but work on either of the two components should interfere only slightly with that on the other. We refer to these components as *modules* within the system.

The essential features of the modular approach can be expressed

---

[1] The claim that *all* systems can be split in this way is open to dispute.

quite simply. The underlying idea is that you break up the design of the system into as many separate modules as possible, and work on these independently. For this process to make sense, two things have to be true.

* *loose coupling*
    decisions made by the designers of one module shouldn't have any major effect on the designs of the others.

* *strong cohesion*
    different parts of a system are included in a single module because decisions about one of the parts cannot sensibly be made without considering their effects on the other. If this isn't the case, the two parts can be regarded as modules in their own right.

**There are other approaches**

Although this course is about modular software design, we would like to stress that it isn't the only way forward, just as SSADM[2] isn't always an appropriate design methodology. Modular software design underlies most modern software development methodologies, and is applicable to most programming languages and implementation techniques. Nonetheless, adopting a modular approach is likely to *increase* the amount of work you carry out during requirements analysis - you have to be certain that the way you carve up a system into modules really makes sense. Modular design isn't a *replacement* for other design methods, it's a system which complements them. Part of the skill of software engineering is learning how to combine methods in the most appropriate way for the

---

[2] SSADM, or Structured Systems Analysis and Design Methodology, is a Government endorsed methodology, suitable for the analysis and design of large paper-based organisations. There have been attempts to make it suitable for team-based organisations, not entirely successfully. The details of SSADM are not relevant to this course.

particular problem in hand.

We begin the course with an overview of the development of large systems, going on to cover the analysis and high-level design phase. Later, we cover detailed design, module specification, and implementation techniques. We conclude with a discussion on the merits of testing.

# Chapter 2

# Large Systems Development

---

Large systems differ from small systems in many ways.
Being bigger, they are also inherently more complex,
requiring co-ordinated effort from a well-managed team
of individuals. Furthermore, large systems always need
fixing or improving.

---

**The classical lifecycle model**

The traditional view of software design and development assumes the familiar waterfall life cycle model, encompassing 6 main stages (*Figure 2.1*) [Fai85].

* *system engineering and analysis*: software is part of a major system, so we need to examine the entire system first, and then decide which bits have to be handled by the software, and which bits by the rest of the system.

* *software requirements analysis*: before you can design something, you need to know what it will be used for. This is a difficult stage, because the customer often doesn't know what's wanted! Documentation of the requirements, both software and hardware, should be discussed with the customer to make sure

you've got it right.

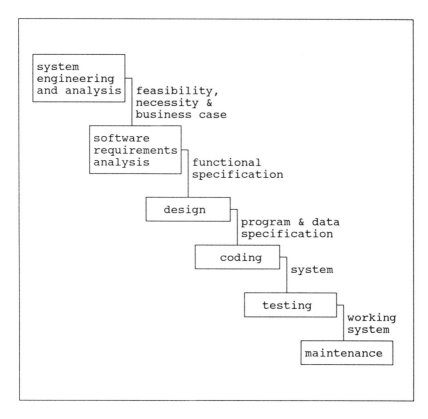

Figure 2.1

* *design*: you've got to work out data structures, the software
  architecture, and procedural details. Once you've got the
  design, you can check it for quality - before coding actually
  starts. Generally speaking, structured design seems to be
  easier to check and maintain than *ad hoc*.

* *coding*: provided your design was clear, translating it into machine readable form should be quite straightforward.

* *testing*: naturally, if the software you're designing is large, you'll expect some mistakes to have been made, so testing is essential. Traditionally, testing is something that is only considered towards the end of the design process, and so can be quite difficult. Hardware designers are more sensible - they design the hardware in such a way that it will be easy to test, a process which requires testing to be considered right at the start of the design process. You should try to do likewise in your design of software.

* *maintenance*: no matter how good your software system is, it will need maintenance throughout its useful lifetime. This can be for a number of reasons. The hardware platform on which the system runs may be upgraded, or perhaps the customer's needs may change significantly. It may be that heavier-than-expected demands may be placed upon the system, so that bottle-necks may have become important. And, of course, it may be that new faults have been discovered that were missed at the testing phase.

**Problems with the classical lifecycle model**

Although the classical life cycle model is quite popular, it has drawbacks, and many software engineers follow quite different strategies altogether. Some observers consider the waterfall model to be 'worse-than-useless', as illustrated by the following remarks [Lev87]

... It evolved as a development method to allow orderly management of the software cycle. The problem that it addressed was the premature coding of programs that would have to be changed as the full requirements of the system became clear ... The waterfall method attempted to solve this problem by applying some resources initially so that when the programs were actually written the time and effort invested would not be wasted.

However, what has happened is precisely the opposite of what was intended. The software that was developed to the requirements and specifications may have met those specifications but did not satisfy the needs of the real users, either because the process of creating requirements and specification is inherently difficult or because the process took so long that the needs changed.

Practical experience shows that customers rarely understand the limitations of software, and software engineers rarely understand the business context of their customers, so misunderstandings can often arise. Add to this the fact that customers rarely know precisely what they want, and it's clear that software design requires much more flexibility than the classical lifecycle model allows.

In addition, classical lifecycle design requires the customer to be extremely patient. They have no way of assessing how far the design process has got until they see the nearly-finished product. A customer - especially a customer for an expensive system - is unlikely to accept the uncertainty and stress that this entails. And what happens if the project takes longer than you've budgeted for? Since you've nothing to show the customer but a few scraps of paper and half-finished code, they're unlikely to be particularly sympathetic to your arguments that all you need is another couple of months.

In any case, the classical lifecycle model doesn't make economic sense! In business, you design a product knowing that it will eventually become obsolete. No product is perfect, and better products will eventually be produced, either by yourself, or your competitors. Even if a product is perfect now, it won't be in the future, because your customer's needs will change. Consequently, the idea of trying to satisfy all of your customer's requirements is bad business sense. You ought to aim to satisfy them over the lifetime of the software as a viable *product* - and this lifetime is determined by the economic pressures of maintaining strategic advantage in what is basically a cut-throat industry. There is no point designing software that will survive a decade, if the need it is to satisfy will disappear within five years.

Finally, we should note that the 'life cycle' is a model of one development phase (development up to the point of delivery) - it fares badly when used to model the *whole* development process (taking into account maintenance and enhancement requirements.

### Evolutionary design and prototyping

There have, of course, been many attempts to get round these problems. Two of the most popular are *rapid prototyping* and *evolutionary design*.

---

**Example 2.2.** Suppose a confectioner has been asked to provide a spectacular birthday cake for a child's birthday party, but that the customer isn't quite sure what 'spectacular' means in this particular case. Only the most confident (or foolish?) of confectioners would produce the cake and then ask if it were acceptable. The more sensible approach would be to develop a collection of possible designs (probably drawn on paper, and perhaps accompanied by a few sample pieces of cake, or photographs of previous commissions), and present them to the customer. The customer can then choose the most acceptable, and add

a few comments like 'can I have this one, but with
larger writing' or 'yes, but wouldn't it be better
with yellow icing and shaped like an aeroplane?' Armed
with this new information, the confectioner can now
produce the cake, or else supply new drawings to the
customer, just in case there are still some areas of
ambiguity to sort out. Only when the design has been
agreed upon by the customer as being precisely what
they'd like will the actual cake be produced.

---

This is an example of *evolutionary* design. The design is never
completely replaced - it is simply upgraded. You start with a simple
prototype (the initial drawing, in this case), use it to obtain more
information about the customer's requirements, and then modify the
prototype. When the prototype is acceptable, you use it as the model on
which to base the *actual* system design.

*Rapid prototyping* is slightly different[1], since the prototype is not
upgraded, but used to elicit information from the customer about missing
or mismatched requirements. Having served this purpose, the prototype is
thrown away, and a new design is produced. There are three common
types of rapid prototyping within software systems design.

* *paper prototypes*: these are like the designs used by the
  confectioner. They let the customer know what the finished
  product will look like, but they don't really do anything else.

* *working prototypes* go a bit further. They let the customer see a
  little more of how the system will respond. The software at this
  stage will usually be far from perfect. For example, the
  algorithms being used may be incredibly inefficient, and entire

---

[1] Authors disagree as to whether evolutionary design and rapid prototyping are or are not different
versions of the same methodology.

sections of the system may be missing.

* *complete prototypes* have all the sections of the system present, but in an inappropriate form. It may run for the small examples that the customer is likely to try out at this stage - just to get a feel for the system - but probably wouldn't be very suitable for the much greater demands that can be expected when the system is finally installed in its correct working environment.

### Problems with prototyping

The essential advantage of prototyping over classical design is the speed with which the customer sees the system developing, which in turn allows any ambiguities in the requirements specification to be ironed out early. Of course, no method is perfect, and prototyping has its own share of problems.

Since the prototype is being used as a requirements gathering tool, the designer will often use inefficient methods in its construction, perhaps employing inappropriate datastructures, algorithms, or even operating systems. After a while, she or her colleagues may have forgotten why those particular choices were made (if they were ever told), and inadvertently assume that they are essential to the system as a whole. The result is a system that performs poorly, and which probably doesn't satisfy the customer.

Then again, once the customer has seen the working prototype, they are likely to assume that it *is* the final system. After all, it seems to work well for the small example runs they've tried out (don't forget, there's no guarantee that the customer is the same person who will eventually have to *use* the system!), so why bother carrying out any further work on the design? If the customer is insistent, the designer may all too often be tempted to give way, and simply carry out a little cosmetic surgery. In the long run, of course, this can be bad for business - if the user becomes too dissatisfied, the customer may be persuaded to shop elsewhere next time.

## Cyclic development

*Cyclic development* has emerged as a hybrid approach, incorporating features from the classical waterfall model, rapid prototyping, and evolutionary design [DaW89]. Each design cycle has its own 'mini' lifecycle, and results in the production of a complete system. Any modification requirements identified from the $n$th cycle are introduced in the $(n+2)$th cycle. In this way, the functionality of the developed system is expanded from cycle to cycle, until a complete 'solution' is developed.

There are several advantages to the cyclic approach, including

* since functionality is being expanded bit by bit, it is easier to keep control of development costs.

* the customer is always guaranteed to get *something* in return for their investment.

* the customer is consulted frequently, minimising the chances of late 'surprises'.

* it costs less to scrap a function, or a partially functional system, than would be the case were the complete system to be developed in its entirety.

* cyclic design encourages efficient usage of skilled personnel, by ensuring that all the participants are involved all the time, albeit on different phases of the system development.

## Maintenance and Formal Design Methods

After you've installed your completed system, your customer will probably expect you to maintain it as well (the cost of this service will usually have been included in your bill). Maintenance is a very costly and time-consuming business, especially if you discover a problem that can only be sorted out by carrying out a major re-design. It has been predicted that without significant changes in the way we design software, a full quarter of all American school leavers will be needed to maintain faulty COBOL code by the beginning of the next millennium.

The question, then, is how to reduce the maintenance demands of your system. One approach is to use *formal design methods*. Again the ideas are quite simple. Much of the work carried out during maintenance simply deals with correcting errors in the original programming. Formal design, with its emphasis on mathematical rigour and verification, seeks to remove this need by ensuring that the system you design is *provably* correct. Currently, formal design methods are insufficiently developed to be of use in all but the smallest or most safety-critical of systems, but once suitable software tools have been developed - probably in the form of CASE-like support environments - we can expect them to become more realistic.[2]

It's important to distinguish between *formal* and *semi-formal* methods. These latter include techniques like JSD, SSADM, Yourdon, Constantine and DeMarco, but are *not* rigourous in the same sense as the logical transformation of Z and VDM specifications into code. Semi-formal methods simply provide a framework in which to design your system; they supply a guiding principle - or in extreme cases an over-detailed checklist - in the hope that, by structuring your thoughts during the design process, you will understand more thoroughly what you're doing.

---

[2] Formal methods suffer from many defects of their own, and cannot fully replace the need for adequate testing of the product. This is discussed in depth later.

Whether you use formal, semi-formal, or *ad hoc* methods, however, the need for maintenance is inescapable. Successful companies need to maintain their competitive advantage over their competitors, and this requires the ability to restructure rapidly. Restructuring of a company and its product and marketing bases entails a re-organisation of its information systems - which means that your system will need modification.

### Modularisation makes maintenance easier

When you come to modify your system, it's likely that most of your system will still be acceptable, with enhancements required to just a few of its component modules. Because you only have to modify modules, the modification process is quicker and cheaper than would be the case if your software were written as a single unit.

---

**Example 2.3.** Spark-plugs are separate modules in a standard engine, and are easy to clean and replace when they become faulty. If they were built-in, the entire engine would be have to be taken out of action.

---

In addition, modularisation makes it easier to *locate* faults. Once a fault is discovered, you can test each module in turn - the loose coupling between modules increases the chances that the faults are entirely contained within single modules, or else in the fairly simple interfaces between modules. And in the worst case - when the module has to be completely replaced, loose coupling comes to your rescue again, since it ensures that any one module can be re-written without affecting the viability of other sections of the system.

**Project teams and project leaders**

Designing a large software system is a team activity, and involves all the problems inherent in all forms of group management. Notice, by the way, that the emphasis is on the word *team*. Any collection of people can form a *group*, but only a team can perform well.

While it is the responsibility of every group member to maintain the vitality of the team, there is often a special individual whose role is to direct the team, and who is ultimately considered responsible for the success or failure of the project team. This team leader - if there is one - will often be imposed on the group by managers elsewhere within the company hierarchy, and there is no guarantee that they will be successful. Groups tend to select their own *informal* leaders, and problems will arise if the 'official' and informal leaders are in conflict. Companies in other industries, notably the car manufacturer Volvo, have found that leaderless teams perform just as well as, and sometimes better than, teams with an imposed hierarchy. But however the team decides to organise itself, some problems will remain.

* From time to time conflicts will arise within the group, which have to be dealt with fairly and quickly.

* Teams are most effective when they are small and specialised [Bro75].

* Members of the team need to know their *role* within the project, and this role must correspond to what they find themselves asked to do. There's no point telling someone that they're in charge if you then undermine their every decision.

* Members have to relinquish control to other members of the team. Many people prefer to see a project through to completion, but this will be incompatible with team working if

their responsibility doesn't extend to the final stages.

* Large systems have significant communications overheads, since contact has to be maintained between the various specialists involved in development, e.g. users, designers, analysts, test teams, financial departments, senior management, and implementors.

## Project planning

In order to get a contract, you will have made guarantees to your customers (which would be your own finance and marketing divisions, in the case of speculative software products). You will have estimated both the costs and likely benefits of the system, and the amount of time needed to develop it. This implies that a great deal of project planning has to take place before the project itself starts, and that a lot of careful control has to be exercised to ensure that you stick to your targets.

Project planning involves two activities, research and estimation. The first step in both the modular and the classical lifecycles focusses on systems analysis: you need to know what the *total* system will be like, of which your software is to be a part. This means that *research* has to be undertaken, both to provide an understanding of this total system, and also to establish precisely where the boundaries of the software component will be drawn, and those of its internal modules. And once the research has been undertaken, you will need to *estimate* how much the project will cost, and how long it will take.

Unfortunately, estimation carries a certain amount of risk with it. First, there is the natural risk associated with any attempt to predict an uncertain future. Any number of uncontrollable events may occur which seriously affect the validity of your estimates, ranging from illness and absenteeism to fluctuations in exchange rates and fiscal policy. Giving a firm estimate in such circumstances requires a great deal of experience, preferably backed up by large supplies of historical information on which to base your decision.

The second problem is more insidious. If you are tendering a bid for a project, and the competition is known to be tough, you will naturally try to make the lowest offer price that you consider sensible. The tendency will be to look on the optimistic side, and this can lead to serious underestimates of the actual economic and time costs. It's a truism in the software engineering world that *every* project runs over-budget and over-time.

**Goals and milestones**

Once the project is agreed as feasible, it needs to be *controlled*. In order to see how well the project is progressing, there have to be targets against which it can be measured. Fairley [Fai85] highlights four types of project goal, reflecting the fact that every project serves not only to produce a system, but also to enhance the skills of the personnel working on it. Goals can either involve the product or the process involved, and can be either quantitative or qualitative. Here are a few examples (*Table 2.4*).

|              | Process | Product |
|--------------|---------|---------|
| Quantitative | The system should be delivered within 12 months | The system should reduce costs by at least 12% |
| Qualitative  | Team members should acquire better understanding of SSADM | Users should find the system more fun to use |

Table 2.4

Once the goals are established, it is common to set project milestones. These take the form of targets that have to be reached by certain times, such as *'phase one should be complete within 5 weeks'*. By matching performance to milestones, the project members can assess how well they are keeping to target, and can identify, early on, whether any major headaches are to be expected. By spotting areas of the project which are lagging behind, or which are generating excessive costs, the team can take remedial action before the situation gets out of hand.

### A final reminder about documentation

We stressed in the introduction that you owe it to your colleagues to keep clear and complete documentation. Documentation comes in many forms, however, and you must ensure that each form of documentation is kept up-to-date. It should be the case that documentation is always sufficiently complete to enable a colleague to take over from you at short notice - for example, if you should be taken ill, or leave for another project or company. Nobody will thank you for leaving things in such a state that they have to start from scratch. Unfortunately, documentation represents possibly the most neglected area of software design, and looks set to remain so. Here's what Levy [Lev87], writing about software economics, has to say about it.

> ... One important area in which I do not see any progress is in the productivity or quality of the documentation. Documentation is a significant part of software, but I see no hopeful signs ... it will require much research to achieve significant results in this area.

# Chapter 3

# Analysis And Design

---

This section addresses the analysis and high level
design of software systems. Analysis is the
definition of user requirements, high level design is
a process of planning how best to meet the user
requirements with modular software components.

---

**Introduction**

In all system development methods there are at least three pre-delivery phases.

* **Analysis:** Understanding the user requirements, stating these requirements and agreeing with the user exactly what is needed. This needs knowledge of the user's environment and the definition of their actual requirements (often these requirements are different to the ones originally stated).

* **Design:** How the user's requirements will be achieved. A transformation of the requirements into a statement of how they will be met; how data will be processed and what constraints and checks need to be applied.

* **Implementation:** A further transformation, this time from the design into a working system using the appropriate system development tools and programming languages.

In short analysis is *what* is needed, design is *how it will be* achieved, and implementation is *how it is* achieved. Software development from analysis through to implementation is a series of transformations from the intangible (hence difficult to define) user requirements into a tangible (hence easy to find fault with) system.

This section will cover the analysis and high level design phases of development. Popular methods of analysis and design will be presented to illustrate the variety of techniques in use commercially. Section 4 addresses detailed design (specification) and implementation details.

**Software Engineering**

Software as an engineering discipline has been a popular goal of academics and industrialists for a number of decades. Since engineering by definition is 'the application of scientific knowledge' the goal of a scientific engineering approach to software development seems most worthy. The shortage of 'scientific knowledge' in software development has led to the adoption of techniques from more traditional engineering disciplines in systems development. The contention is that developing a computer system should be a disciplined well ordered process similar to building a bridge , a sports stadium or an integrated circuit.

The appeal of a disciplined engineering approach probably stems from the abundance of examples of houses, factories, cars, aircraft etc. that are built on time, to budget and that meet the user requirements. Whereas examples of software systems on time, within budget and meeting the user requirements are rare. One of the key problems with software development that causes delays and overspent budgets is failure to meet the user requirements or not clearly understanding the user requirements when tendering for the work and therefore having to do far more work than anticipated to deliver a satisfactory system.

The engineering approach to this problem is to clearly define the users requirements and then agreeing how these requirements will be met. An engineer commissioned to build a bridge would first find out where the bridge needed to be, then how much traffic it needed to carry and any special requirements such as elevating to allow for boats to pass underneath. Once the requirements were agreed, the engineer would draw up some plans based on other bridge designs and information such as metal strengths, car weights etc. From these plans, artists impressions or models could be made so that the more detailed features of the bridge could be agreed with the user. At this point the work can be planned and the bridge built. The bridge engineer has a number of advantages over a software engineer:

* Bridge building has been around for hundreds of
  years and therefore the engineer has a lot of
  historical precedents to learn from.

* The user (even the most unsophisticated user) has a
  good understanding of what a bridge is and the
  function that it should perform.

* Estimating the cost of bridge building is fairly
  straightforward since each job has been done before
  and is therefore of a known cost (some scaling may
  need to be employed).

The software engineer needs to try to use the same techniques as the bridge builder quite often with few (if any) similar systems upon which to base the design or cost estimates. The users will generally find it difficult to specify (or even know) their requirements and will find it difficult to visualise the system being proposed. The analysis and design phases of the project therefore must provide an environment in which the user can develop a clear understanding of their requirements (agreeing to them) and understand the nature of the system that has been designed for them. User involvement is essential in developing acceptable software on time and within budget. This may sound obvious but too often commercial software is presented to the user after spending much more than the allocated budget and the user can't use it and more to the point didn't even want it ! This is made worse by the analyst quite often having to deal with at least three 'users'; the user representative who participates in the early discussions and controls the use of the system (may never go near it in practice), the owner who 'sponsors' or pays for the system generally a senior manager (will almost certainly never go near the system) and finally the user who operates the system (uses it constantly but is unlikely to be consulted prior to system installation).

Other engineering methods such as estimating cost based on previous similar work are now being used in software development. Quite a lot of interest has been shown in software development metrics [DeM87] in recent years in an effort to establish a scientific measurement basis for estimation and control of development tasks, these methods are still in their infancy and are not in general use.

Not all techniques adopted from engineering have served to improve software production, some of the project control methods inherited from construction projects have resulted in experienced analysts, programmers and designers becoming entrenched in a planning bureaucracy that prevents them from adding value to the development process and thus raises software development cost. The level of control needed on a construction project with 100 contractors is often unwieldy when applied to development teams of 5 or 6 but still needs a planner to do it.

The cause of software engineering has progressed considerably over the past two decades and a professional engineering approach to development is becoming far more common in industry.

## Analysis

Analysis as previously stated, is the definition of requirements for a particular system. The main deliverable of the analysis phase is a specification of user requirements for the proposed system, this is often called the Functional Specification. The Functional Specification states in detail what the project will deliver ie. what the system will do. This document will be agreed with the user (generally the one who will pay for the system) and will provide the starting point for the design and implementation phases. Details such as costs, benefits, schedules, acceptance testing and performance estimates may be included in this specification.

Returning to the earlier bridge building example, the Functional Specification for a bridge will probably be along the lines of:

```
A bridge from A to B, four lanes wide, capable of
carrying 2500 vehicles per hour .......
```

Obviously the level of detail would be a lot greater but the 'user' could probably visualise the proposed bridge and decide if it would be satisfactory. Contrast this with a paint manufacturer who wants a 'stock control system'. A few questions that immediately spring to mind are:

```
Is the system to monitor paint in the warehouse
ready to sell or all the raw materials through the
production process?
```

What current manual procedures will be affected by
the system ?

Will the system provide automated ordering of raw
materials ?

Are invoices to be automatically produced ?

Is a computer system really necessary ?

The 'user' is unlikely to know the answers to all the above questions and certainly not to all the subsequent questions. From the broad requirement of 'a stock control system' a set of detailed system requirements needs to be defined and presented in a way that the user can visualise the proposed system as clearly as they would be able to visualise a proposal for a four lane suspension bridge. An additional complication is that the users requirements will change over time (this is a fundamental law of analysis), therefore the specification has to be highly maintainable and capable of straightforward modification.

The analysis of requirements for a computer systems is a complex task requiring a clear understanding of the target environment for the system and clear, effective communication with the interested parties in the development (users, developers, sponsors etc.). Once defined, the requirements must be presented in a palatable form to the interested parties and agreed (by the person or persons paying the bill).

A popular approach to analysis is 'structured analysis' developed in the late seventies and later adopted by the developers of prescriptive methods such as SSADM [Cut87,DCC88]. Often an analyst will use a hybrid approach, using a number of techniques (some formal, others less so, some sheer guess-work) depending on the type of system (control,

'Users' are more familiar with some things ...

... than they are with others.

database, safety critical etc.) and the environment ('greenfield' site, automating manual procedures, upgrading existing system).

## Structured analysis

Structured analysis is aimed at producing a structured system specification (Functional Specification), DeMarco [DeM78] suggests that a structured specification needs to have the following qualities:

* It should be graphic. Using data flow diagrams to show clearly what is being specified.

* It should be partitioned. Providing a smooth transition from high level abstraction to low level detail.

* It should be rigourous. A data dictionary specifies the interfaces between processes while the process definitions describe the transformations.

* It should be maintainable. Changes can be made in a controlled, straightforward way. The impact of changes are therefore clear, making it simple to determine the economy of proposed modifications.

* It should be iterative. By using graphic representation and partitioning into manageable sections, the user can participate in the development of the specification. The 'user review - analyst correction' cycle needs to be repeated until a section is approved. The approved section will then form part of the specification.

* It    should    be    logical    rather    than    physical.
  Implementation details such as hardware, vendor etc.
  need to be eliminated from the development of the
  specification    if    possible.    This    allows    the
  essential   logical   processing   requirements   to   be
  defined without being influenced by irrelevant (at
  this stage) implementation detail.

* It should be precise, concise and readable.  As with
  all system documentation the quality rather than the
  quantity of the finished specification is important.

The tools used in building this specification are:

* data flow diagrams:  In their simplest form data flow
  diagrams consist of four symbols; the *named vector*
  (data   flow)   showing   a   data   path,   the   *bubble*
  (process) portraying a transformation of data, the
  *straight line* showing a file or a data base and the
  *box* (a source or sink) which is an external entity.

  These data flow diagrams are used to model the
  processing of data in the domain of the required
  system.   They   are   used   in   user   discussions   to
  clarify understanding and are reviewed by the user.
  Data    flow    diagrams    show    errors    as    glaring,
  indefensible errors and as such are a useful model
  once validated.

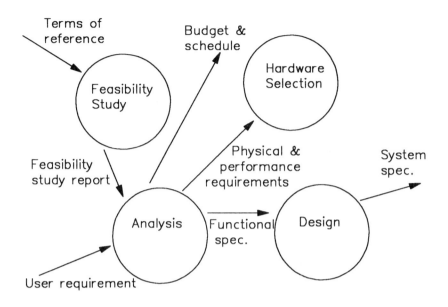

# DFD for Analysis Phase

*data dictionary: In data flow diagrams, the data
flows are labelled simply and uniquely. A data flow
labelled 'customer pid' intuitively suggests that
details of the customers name, address etc. are
moving between processes. The definition of
'customer pid' is held in the data dictionary
possibly as 'surname + initials + address +
telephone', 'address' is probably another definition
in the dictionary. The data dictionary provides a
rigourous definition of each data flow.

This detailed knowledge of the composition of
data flow is used to understand the data present in

the environment and to eliminate data redundancy and duplication.

* structured English:  each process (data transform) in a data flow diagram needs to be described.  The most common  approach  is  to  use  structured  English. Structured English is clear, unambiguous, brief but sufficient for the purpose.  It is constructed from three  logical  constructs;  *sequence*  -  action statement(s) applied one after the other without interruption, *repetition* - action(s) done over and over within some limit, and *decision* - two or more actions only one of which is applied in a particular case.  Indentation  of  text  is  used  to  show  the nesting of the various constructs.  The advantage of such a structured language subset is that the user will be able to understand it without training and there is no room for individual interpretation.

```
IF the construct is a decision
THEN
        FOR EACH construct that is a repetition

        do the first sequential item

        do the next sequential item
OTHERWISE
        do the sequential item here
```

*Figure 3.4. Structured English*

Decision tables [Gil70] and decision trees [War74] are also used when the selection of an action depends upon a number of conditions.

Walkthrough techniques are used extensively throughout the analysis phase to ensure the validity and acceptability of the requirements being defined.

Once a satisfactory set of data flow diagrams (with the appropriate data dictionary and process definitions) of the current environment (which may be an existing system or the user view of a proposed new system) has been produced, they are refined into a logical model. This logical model is derived by normalising [Dat81] the file structures and minimising data flow. Once the logical system has been agreed then the logical requirements can be factored into the data flow diagrams, which are then expanded to a required physical model which is the central part of the structured specification.

The structured specification will contain items other than the data flow diagrams showing the processes and data required to fulfil the user requirements. Items such as interface details, error messages, startup / shutdown procedures, acceptance testing and performance will probably be covered. The inclusion of interface and error message formats in the analysis rather than design phase may seem odd at first, but the interface is viewed as one of the most important user requirements and is the one they are best able to judge. It is the approach to screen layout and error messages will be agreed at this stage rather than detailed layouts or messages. Having the user understand and agree to the interface design approach as part of the functional specification avoids many iterations of screen design close to installation.

The methods and techniques of structured design have been incorporated into modern larger methodologies such as SSADM. The analysis phase in SSADM is similar to the original structured analysis, the major difference being an imposition of structure, defining stages and tasks. The data flow diagrams symbols used in SSADM are different to the 'bubble' diagrams described earlier and contain a little more information. Entity modelling is carried out in conjunction with producing data flow diagrams and the two models are cross referenced for validation, Entity Life Histories (ELH) are produced from this cross reference matrix and are used later in the logical process design. There is a formal proposal of system options, a system selection and formal setting of design constraints. The major deliverable of the analysis phase remains a 'signed off' specification of requirements.

Structured analysis provides a well proven framework for producing the key Functional Specification document. Unfortunately, because analysis is indefinite (it is impossible to exhaustively define user requirements in a changing environment) and requires considerable interpersonal skills, the analysis phase is shortened and design is started too early (or worse still coding follows the 'analysis' phase). The recent widespread use of SSADM and similar prescriptive methodologies should encourage the completion of a sound analysis phase. The increasing complexity of modern business intensifies the need for sound business and systems analysis to provide cost beneficial computer systems, competitive market forces have made business less tolerant of computer systems that do not meet requirements.

## Design

The analysis phase produces a detailed, agreed functional specification of the system and a model of the process and data to be included in the system. The specification delivered to the designers is unlikely to remain static and therefore the analyst continues to play an active role defining and clarifying user objectives and requirements. Analysis is generally an indefinite exercise, needing compromise and negotiation to achieve an agreement of requirements. Design, on the other hand, should be a straightforward (yet skilled) transformation of requirements into a definite, precise plan of how they will be achieved using a program or set of programs.

Design requires considerable skill to produce the plan of how the requirements will be met. Design as addressed in this section is the production of a model of how the system will be structured on a large scale based on relatively abstract objects (modules). The high level system design will define the modules (functional components) that will make up the system and the interfaces between them. The detailed design phase (specification) is where the internal working of these modules is defined this phase is addressed in the next section.

The major deliverables of the high level design phase are logical descriptions of processes and their interrelationships. These descriptions must be at a level that can be expanded to describe detailed physical processing. There are a large number of methods that can be used in the design phase to represent the modular composition of the system, some of the more commonly used approaches will be described here to show different approaches to the design task. The representation and validation of design will also be considered. Module selection and the structure of programs will be examined in section 5.

## Top-down decomposition

This approach emphasises the function that a program and its constituent parts will perform. The program is described in abstract terms and then broken down into levels of lesser abstraction resulting in a level of functional components or modules. The resulting design model is the familiar inverted tree structure.

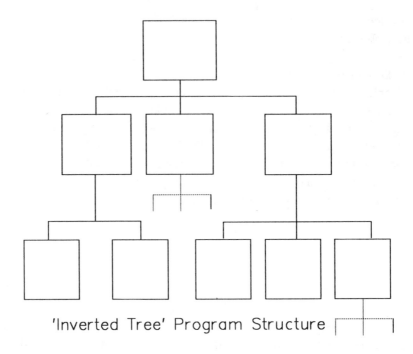

*Figure 3.5*

The high level modules will be abstract e.g. 'spell check', at the middle levels detail will increase e.g. 'read line' and at the lower levels definite 'atomic' actions will be performed e.g. 'read character'.

The intuitive nature of the top-down approach has led to it being widely used but has also resulted in a lack of an accepted method for performing functional decomposition. Decisions such as at what level to end the decomposition and which low level modules should be combined are often based on experience.

A refinement of Top-down decomposition, decomposition based on data flow was developed from the work of Constantine [YoC79] and is a method for transforming data flow diagrams produced by structured design into hierarchical structure charts.

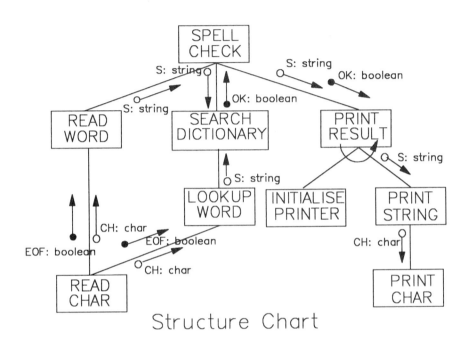

Structure Chart

## Data centred design

Design methods produced by Jackson [Jac75] are used to design program structure based on the structure of data. Jackson Structured Programming (JSP) and Jackson Structured Design (JSD) are the most widely known of the data centred methods. JSP notation (structure diagrams) is used for representing data structure, high level program structure and detailed program design.

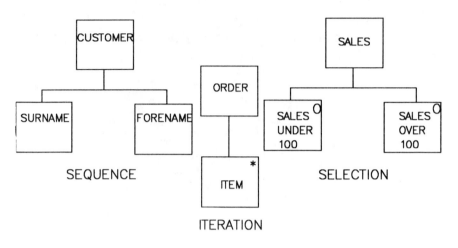

JSP / JSD Chart Components

*Figure 3.7*

The basic idea is to construct a tree to represent the data structure and then to construct the program by developing a structure that corresponds directly to the data structure. The direct mapping from data to program makes modification to the design caused by changes in data structure relatively straightforward.

Jackson data centred design begins with tree structures representing the logical input data and the required output data, both of which are defined in the analysis phase. A similar diagram is then produced for a program that is a composite of these two. Operations are then allocated to the program tree that act on the data in the corresponding positions in the data charts. Intermediate files are used when a direct correspondence between the input and output data structures does not exist.

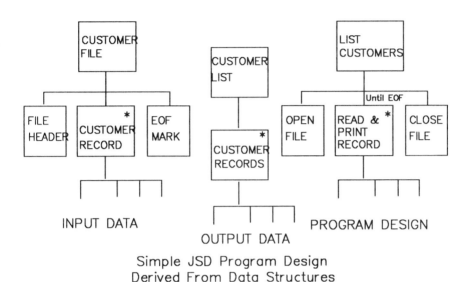

Simple JSD Program Design
Derived From Data Structures

*Figure 3.8*

An important point about the Jackson program structure charts is that each level is processed sequentially from left to right and therefore the program diagrams show both process and sequence information.

Jackson design methods are obviously better suited to data processing applications rather than process control, however the lower level JSP detailed program specifications are applicable for specifying programs in any procedural language.

**Object Oriented Design (OOD)**

Object methods are based on the idea that computer systems can be built as a set of software models of the 'real world' processes it is performing. The object (e.g. customer) consists of attributes / data (e.g. name, address) and all the actions appropriate to that data (e.g. create, modify, delete) and are implemented as a single system component. Constructing systems from such objects provides high modularity.

Object oriented programming (OOPS) has recently attracted considerable attention within the computer industry. Object oriented programming and the associated design methods have generated interest in recent years mainly because of their use in relation to graphical user interfaces (GUI's) such as Microsoft Windows, Presentation Manager and the Apple Macintosh Interface. Although referred to as programming, OOPS introduces important design concepts that are significant in many areas of software development.

Extravagant claims have been made of the benefits of OOPS, some realistic benefits usually attributed to OOPS are:

* Improved software quality

* Increased development productivity

* Reduced project dependences

These are achieved through:

* Developing software that closely represents the problem being solved

* The ability to reuse large amounts of software.

* OOPS requiring totally modular software design.

In order to discuss object oriented design some of the basic jargon of OOPS will be introduced.

An *object* is a systems environment in which data and the mechanisms whereby that data is manipulated are encapsulated within a 'black box' - the object.

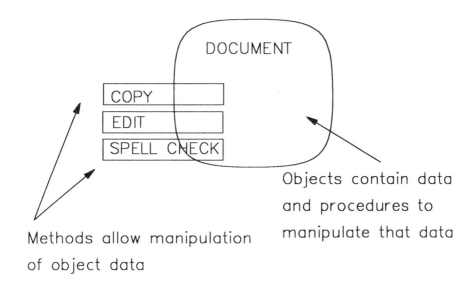

Objects and Methods

*Figure 3.9*

An example of a software object that models a 'real world' item is a word processing document, examples of the object data would be the document text, creation date, file size, modification date etc. The code inside the object could be to amend the text, create a new document, perform a spelling check etc. An actual document exists as an object with its own data. If more than one document were to be manipulated by the system there would be a document object for each one, they would be presented and manipulated separately.

The only way to alter the object's data is via *methods* (procedures) such as edit and spell check. A method is activated by passing a *message* (procedure call) to the object asking it to perform an action on itself e.g. sending the document a message to perform a spelling check would cause the spell check method to be performed.

This object structure provides a totally modular programming environment.

In the real world, objects (documents, bank accounts, cars, trees, dogs) generally do not exist as isolated occurrences that are unrelated to other objects. They fall into sets of objects that share some attributes and behaviour e.g. sports cars, evergreen trees, interest bearing bank accounts.

This grouping of objects into sets with common attributes and behaviour is known in OOPS as *classification*. Objects in a *class* inherit data structure (attributes) and methods (behaviour) from a typical object that defines the class. This *inheritance* is an important concept of OOPS. Objects that inherit class behaviour are defined by their difference to the class rather than as a completely new entity.

To illustrate the idea of classes and inheritance, the document example can be expanded. A document is a type of file and therefore could inherit some attributes such as creation date, size etc. from a general 'file class', program files would also share some of the attributes of this 'file class'. Word processing documents and program objects are therefore defined only by their difference from the general 'file class' ie. word processing documents can be spelling checked, programs can be executed. The common behaviour, ie. all files can be copied or deleted, is only defined as part of the 'file class' and the code to perform these actions (and sometimes data structure) is reused by the more specialised objects such as document and program. This inheritance of data structure and behaviour is a common feature of object systems.

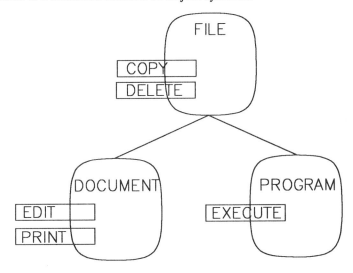

## Classes and Inheritance

*Figure 3.10*

This classification of related items, that inherit from a general object and are refined by difference is central to OOPS. This provides the mechanism whereby large amounts of code may be reused.

Object oriented methodology has been described as the second great programming revolution, top-down modular structured programming being the first. This may be something of an over statement, given that much of the strengths of object orientation come from its use of totally modular elements. Object oriented programming and design techniques are however becoming a very significant influence on modern software development methods.

The design of object based systems is generally based on entity or data models since objects are abstractions of data rather than function. Booch [Boo86] presents a review of principles used in object-oriented design and describes how object systems can be designed using JSD as a starting point. OOD is object-centred rather than data-centred as in JSD, data is a starting point in defining objects since the data defines the entities and attributes that make an object ie. name and address are attributes of the customer. The design process also needs to associate the operations and processes associated with each object.

A typical approach to OOD consists of the following steps:

* Identify objects and their attributes: entity modelling techniques are used to define the entities (logical data structures), their properties and interrelationships. Entities are generally identified by nouns and attributes by adjectives in a system description.

* Identify the operations performed by or to each object: ELH techniques are suitable for this in that they show the logical processes applied to an entity. The operations are the verbs and adverbs in a description of the system. Objects can be classed as *actors* (performs operations), *servers* (suffers operations) or  *agents* (performs and suffers actions). An operation can be classified as a *constructor* (alters the object state), a *selector* (inspects the current state) or an *iterator* (examines and / or changes state).

* Establish the hierarchy of objects: based on the entity model a hierarchical definition of objects used by other objects is produced e.g. a 'sales invoice' object may use the 'customer' object to provide a postal address.

* Establish the interface to each object: The object is specified in terms of its name and its exports (data items available to other objects).

* Implement each object: the implementation is irrelevant to all but the implementor (and their successor !) since an object is a totally modular item, only its stated function and its interface are important.

Object-oriented programming [DaW89] provides a totally modular implementation method. Currently object based design is a mixture of bottom-up, top-down and data centred design and lacks a widely used structured method. OOPS is rapidly gaining popularity among developers and therefore designs and development techniques will increasingly need to adapt to reflect the OOPS principles of information hiding and modelling 'real-world' items.

## Walkthroughs and Reviews

Throughout the development cycle, there is a need to validate the work done to date. In the analysis phase the model of the users environment needs to be reviewed with the user (probably many times) and the requirements need to be agreed. In the design phase the high level design has to be matched with the requirements and has to be refined. During specification and implementation, the specifications and code need to be validated. All of these items of work require reviews or walkthroughs to ensure their correctness. Formal walkthroughs will be considered in relation to testing in section 6, the general ideas of validation and reviews will be discussed here.

Reviews of work are a fairly informal process, in their simplest form it is asking a colleague to 'have a read through' a report or to check the logic of a structure chart, program tree or data flow diagram.

During the analysis phase it is necessary to review the data flow diagrams (if that is the method used) with the user, this can be extremely productive in clearly defining the user environment, it is important to explain the notation and allow the user time to adjust to using the diagrams.  Once users understand such diagrams they are usually very helpful and embarrassingly good at spotting errors.

Informal reviews of work are very productive and should be used whenever possible in order to trap errors as early as possible. Development teams should review each others work regularly to maintain awareness of other work being carried out in the team and to provide an environment where ideas, help and advice are always available.  The more common reviews are, the more collective accountability the team has for the work of the team.

Formal reviews or walkthroughs are generally for work that is near to completion (or at least was thought complete prior to the walkthrough). There are generally formal attendance requirements and reporting procedures for walkthroughs and the reports form part of project documentation.  General attributes of product reviews or walkthroughs are:

* The participants have prepared by reading/analysing the product (code, data flow diagrams, design etc.).

* A report is produced of modifications required.  Modification detail is not discussed in the review.

* A date is set for the completion of modifications and either someone is designated to 'sign off' the changes or another review is planned.

* Once the review has been conducted the quality of the product is viewed as the collective responsibility of the reviewers rather than the originator.

Each major deliverable in all phases of development must be product reviewed.

Reviews, both formal and informal, when approached properly contribute considerably to overall product quality.

## Computer Aided Software Engineering (Case)

The use of graphical methods in analysis and design such as data flow diagrams, entity life histories, structure charts etc. has only really been popular with developers since the appearance of software to help in the production of such diagrams.

The use of software packages to support the use of a software development technique or a phase of software development is increasing. There are large numbers of packages available (so many that it's difficult to believe that they are all used) that cover practically all development phases.

The definition of what makes a package a CASE tool is vague. An 'Upper CASE' tool generally supports analysis and high level design functions such as drawing data flow diagrams and entity life histories, creating file definitions etc. A 'Lower CASE' tool will support detailed design, specification and may also generate code. Some packages cover the entire development from analysis through to code generation.

The impact of CASE tools in industry is not yet clear. The major success stories have been in 'greenfield' sites and mainly with database applications where software tools have been used to generate large applications in relatively short periods. The use of tools like Automate+ and Excelerator to produce data flow diagrams, process descriptions etc. that are then passed on to manual implementors has provided some productivity gains. These gains are possibly because the arrival of the

CASE package introduced formal analysis and design phases to environments where they did not exist previously.

A report published by the Butler Cox Productivity Enhancement Programme (1990) stated that projects using structured techniques supported by CASE tools had 15% lower than average productivity and 40% above average error rates. The problem was attributed to poor choice of tools and badly managed integration of the tools into the software development environment. However, screen painting tools and walkthrough techniques showed a reduction of 35% to 40% in development effort.

Screen painters, report packages and 4th generation languages are often associated with CASE products but are more logically considered along side other implementation technology (This is discussed in more detail in *Chapter 4*).

# Chapter 4

# Specification & Implementation

---

Specification occurs at every level of the design
process. In the present context, it is used to mean
the extension of the design plan into detailed process
descriptions. Implementation is the conversion of the
specification into a working system.

---

## Specification

Specification occurs at every level of the design process; techniques and methods used at one point of the development process can often be re-applied at a lower level. Accordingly, we have chosen to discuss specification *in general* throughout this *Chapter*. The guiding principle during detailed design is that, whichever specification methods you choose to adopt, no unanswered questions of functionality can be allowed to remain. We have reached a stage where our major concern is a solid, visible product.

## The problem with formal specification

Like the classical 'waterfall' model of software design, formal methods arose in response to the prevailing software crisis of the 1960s, and sought to place software design on a sound theoretical footing.[1] The result has been a proliferation of cryptically entitled mathematical specification languages, each seeking to facilitate system design within its own sphere of application. The ultimate claim in each case can be expressed something like this: *if you use my specification methodology, the system you design will be perfect (or at least better than it would have been otherwise).*[2]

In software engineering, as in life, you should treat all such claims with caution. What *is* perfection in this case?

Software quality is determined by a large number of distinct features, a few of which are shown in *Chart 2.1* below, compiled from taxonomies in [Mye79,GMP88,BiB88]. The formal methods community is predominantly concerned with only one of these aspects - *reliability*. That is, we seek to give a resounding 'yes' to the question '*does the product do what it ought to do?*'. One area in which formal design methods are considered most important is in the design of *safety-critical* systems, those systems where failure entails significant risk of death to those (humans) in the system's environment.[3]

A popular approach is to specify the intended behaviour of the system in terms of *pre-* and *post-conditions*. This view pre-supposes that you can actually describe the *state* of the system in some way, and allows you to specify what the effect of certain operations upon that state ought to be.

---

[1] There is a long-running dispute as to whether the formalists have gone too far. Barron [Bar89] complains "... it is certain that many academic computer scientists have lost sight of the fact that computing should be fun ... the new mandarins ... find their satisfaction (and fun?) in wrestling with abstract specifications and proofs: not for them the joys of actually making things happen, of taming these complex mechanisms to their will".

[2] MPS: Even though I class myself as a formalist, I cannot subscribe to the view that formality is the panacea that will cure all ills in the software industry. There seems to be a wide-spread misunderstanding, even within the theoretical computer science community itself, as to the real limitations of the methods we're developing.

[3] Technically, a system where failure is likely to lead to economic or ecological disaster is *not* regarded as safety-critical, even though the secondary effects may cause human death. We trust you will exercise due caution in all circumstances, regardless of the definitions.

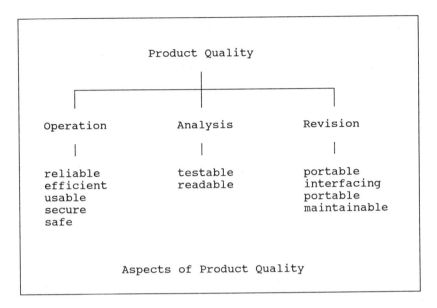

Chart 4.1

**Example 4.2.** Suppose that the system is a word-processor, the state of which is represented by the current contents of a file. The operation we have in mind is deleting some text. Clearly, this isn't possible if the text we want to delete isn't in the file in the first place. So a sensible *pre-condition* for the *delete* operation is that the specified text is present (and the correct occurrence is clearly identifiable, if there is more than one). When we delete the text nothing unexpected should happen at the same time. So our *post-condition* might be something to the effect that "the file looks exactly as it did before, except that the specified text is now missing".

In such circumstances, however, the pre/post-condition approach can generate additional problems if used incorrectly. For example, (a mathematical version of) the following conditions (*Specification 4.3*) might be listed in the specification of a safety-critical system.

```
{PRE:   Water_In_Kettle}

        Put_on(Kettle);

{POST:  Water_Ready_For_Coffee}
```

*Specification 4.3*

This specification tells us something about the properties of kettles, water and coffee, and is the sort of thing a designer might write down when trying to specify the system as it ought to behave. From a safety-critical point of view, however, it is unacceptable since it doesn't tell us what happens when the pre-condition *isn't* satisfied. For safety, we need to know, for each action/pre-condition pair, what happens under both eventualities. A complete specification would, presumably, look something like *Specification 4.4*.

```
{PRE:   Coolant_in_place}

        Put_on(Reactor_Core}

{POST: Power_Available}
{FAIL: Reactor_Explodes}
```

*Specification 4.4*

It's worth mentioning three further difficulties, since these are the problems you are most likely to face yourselves.

* Conversion of a verbal specification into the mathematical format required by these methods requires both skill and patience, and neither can be acquired quickly.

* Until you have a thorough understanding of your customer's business context, you are unlikely to produce a specification that correct matches their requirements.

* Specifying a system formally is pointless, unless you then go on to *prove* that the operations you define actually preserve the designated system invariants. Unfortunately, the mechanics of mathematical proof are notoriously inexact. There are many examples of incorrect programs that have been 'proven' correct, and conversely of correct programs that have (mistakenly) been declared faulty [Las89,GoG75].

It follows, of course, that the use of formal methods doesn't reduce the need for sensible system testing. We shall address this problem further in *Section 6*.


**Structured specification**

Throughout this course, and in conjunction with these lectures, you've been designing a small system (*Appendix A*). It is unlikely, though not impossible, that you opted to use formal methods for this problem, preferring some more graphical technique. This is acceptable.

It is generally accepted that pictures convey more information, and do so more effectively, than formal specifications, *from the point of view of the customer/designer*. This isn't surprising. Theoretical methods are tedious to implement by hand precisely because they are designed to be semi-automatic. Ultimately, the designer should be able to produce the initial specification, and have the resultant code produced by an appropriate software tool.[4]

For the less mathematically minded, and for those working under artificially stringent constraints, it is possible to produce specifications through *structured analysis* [You82], the documentation tools of which include

* structured English

* data flow diagrams (DFDs)

* data structure diagrams (DSDs)

* data dictionaries.

*Structured English* (or French, or whatever) is used whenever we try to describe the step-by-step behaviour of an algorithm in natural language (at lower levels, structured English is often known as *pseudocode*). For example a structured English description of a simple telephone number look-up system for BT's *directory enquiries* might read like *Example 4.5*.

In general, structured English is something like a cross between ordinary English and a programming language. Like the latter, we only allow the use of a limited vocabulary; we need enough words to ensure that the description is readable, but not so many that the description starts to become ambiguous because of double-meanings. But we also allow moments of laxity, where informal phrases like '*we haven't found the number yet*' are inserted into the description to aid clarity (see *Example 4.5* below). Nonetheless, the hallmark of structured English is that it *is* structured - it's easy to point out the appropriate 'sub-specifications' corresponding to different cases that might arise during operation of the

---

[4] MPS: I call this mythical tool the "Sad T Cafe", both in remembrance of the tears likely to be shed before it can become generally available, and also as an acronym for the design approach with which it is likely to be associated (Structured Abstract Data Type Computer Aided Formal Engineering).

system, e.g. what happens if none of the people with the right name live at an address that's familiar to the caller?

```
IF the name appears in the directory
THEN

        FOR EACH occurrence of this name

            check the listed address with the caller;

            IF address is correct
            THEN
                    give the number;
                    end the session (number has been found)

(Getting this far means we haven't found the number yet)

End the session (no such subscriber listed)
```

*Example 4.5*

*Data flow diagrams* (DFDs) show the way information is shunted around the system while it's being processed. For example, let's expand the *directory enquiries* example a little further. Suppose that a customer wants the operator to connect him to a second subscriber, but can't remember the number. Then the flow of information around (some of) the system might be represented as in *Figure 4.6*.

Of course, data flows can be occur at all levels within the system. In this DFD, for example, the unit labelled *Directory Enquiries* represents an entire section of the telephone company's operations. It could, if required, be expanded to a more complete representation, but this would probably make the description somewhat harder to understand.

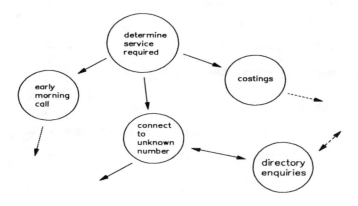

*Figure 4.6*


*Data structure diagrams* are slightly different. Rather than showing how data flows around the system, they show how the different types of data are related to each other. For example, each telephone subscriber has several items of information associated with them, e.g.

```
* type
    is it a personal or business subscriber?
* name and address
* number
    is it listed or unlisted?
    is it currently engaged?
* outstanding charges
```

A data structure diagram for part of this collection of items might look like this.

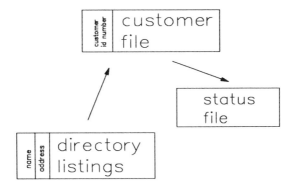

*Figure 4.7*

This diagram tells us that relationships exists between telephone subscribers, their numbers, names and addresses, and their 'status'. In this simple example, each customer has a unique name and address, and each customer file has a unique identification number attached to it. The arrow between *directory listings* and *customer file* indicates that every listing is associated with one or more customer files, and also that we can access this information if we know either of the two **key** values *name* or *address*. The

arrow between *customer file* and *status* tells us that each customer file has
one or more status values associated with it, and that these can be accessed
provided we know the relevant identification number.

The final element of structured specification is the *data dictionary*.
This is simply a list of all the logical relationships between the various
types of data in our system. For example, a few of the data elements in the
telephone system might be defined as follows

```
Subscriber_Information = {Line_Information} +
                         Personal_Details +
                         Outstanding_Charges

Line_Information       = Number +
                         Listing_Status +
                         Engaged_Status

Personal_Details       = Name +
                         Address

Engaged_Status         = ["busy"|"free"|"out_of_order"]
```

*Definitions 4.8*

These entries tell us that every subscriber has the following information
associated with them: details of their outstanding charges and personal
details, and information concerning *one or more* lines. Each line has the
following entries associated with it: a number, information as to whether
it's listed or unlisted, and information as to its *engaged status*. The latter
can take one of three values: *busy, free,* or *out_of_order.* Data dictionaries
can usually be read without difficulty, which is just as well, since a typical
system may contain several thousand such definitions. The notation as we
use it has the following meaning.

```
A = B + C      A consists of B and C
A = {B}        A consists of one or more B's
A = [B|C]      A consists of B or C (not both)
A = (B)        The occurrence of B is optional
```

*Definitions 4.9*

Structured specification is ideally suited (apart from its informality) to top-down design, since it embodies an inherently top-down philosophy. We saw this above, in the definition of *Line_Information*, where the details of sub-items like *Engaged_Status* could be left until later. By using a mixture of data flow diagrams, data structure diagrams, structured English, and data dictionaries, you should find it relatively easy to specify even quite complicated systems in terms that both you and your customer can understand. Structured specification has utility, in that its use forces you think carefully about the system in a highly structured way - thus making subsequent conversion of the specification into a mathematically rigourous description somewhat easier than might otherwise have been the case.[5,6]

## Implementation

Implementation is more than just producing a piece of code. This section deals with *issues* involved in implementing a system. It does not cover actual programming languages, although you may like to evaluate our comments in the light of your own experiences. The points we shall cover include

---

[5] However, lest you had forgotten, while modular design is often top-down, it need not be. There are lessons to be learnt from the development of modularism in industry (see the *Appendix* at the end of this *Section*).

[6] You are probably familiar with other styles of structured specification. You should not interpret our concentration on this approach as meaning that the others are worthless. The role of this discussion is to explain the ideas involved, not necessarily to give a complete overview of all possible methods.

* language considerations

* implementation strategies

* psychological factors

This material necessarily overlaps to some extent with that of *Section 5* ("Structure and Style"), where you will be introduced to further factors, including design complexity, readability, house styles and standards. In addition, implementation styles directly influence testing and maintenance procedures, and these will be considered in depth in *Section 6*.


## Implementation strategies

Depending on the style of specification you have adopted, there are several implementation strategies available to you.

Formalists are able to generate code by means of a process of gradual *refinement* (also called *reification*), during which the specification is slowly transformed from top-level mathematics into implementation-level code. At each refinement step, the mathematician involved has to *prove* that the essential 'meaning' of the specification has been preserved. One feature of especial relevance to this course is the ability to split a specification into several interfacing sub-specifications, which can then be reified individually, thus creating a system which is inherently modular (checks also have to be made to ensure that interface properties are preserved). A comprehensive analysis of these techniques requires considerably more time than is available for this course. You are referred to [Dro89,Mor90] for more details.

If you have adopted a modular design strategy, there are two traditional approaches available to you: top-down and bottom-up construction.

**Top-down construction** assumes that the 'calling sequence' of the modules in your system forms a directed acyclic graph. That is, modules mustn't be called, however indirectly, by modules which they themselves call (if this were to happen, it would be impossible to say which of the two modules lies 'above' the other in the hierarchy). Allowing for this restriction, top-down construction requires you to start by constructing the module at the 'top' of the hierarchy, then those in the next layer, and so on. While this is an intuitively popular approach, it renders testing extremely difficult, since we are not always able to predict precisely how lower modules will behave under all circumstances. A further problem arises when trying to test modules that lie above the input/output module, since we have no means of interacting with them.

**Bottom-up construction** also requires the calling sequence to contain no loops, for the same reason. In this case, we begin by constructing the lowest level modules (those which call no further modules), and gradually move up the hierarchy. Testing is simpler for bottom-up than top-down testing, since we can simulate higher-level modules with some confidence. Unfortunately, however, bottom-up construction cannot begin until the design process is complete, whereas top-down construction allows construction of high-level modules to occur alongside the design of the lower levels.

In general, neither of these approaches can be adopted in their pure form, since calling sequences need not form directed acyclic graphs. In particular, much of the power of modern languages comes through their support of recursive constructs. However, modules which invoke themselves recursively violate the necessary restriction on calling sequences. Under such circumstances a common sense approach is required.

## Incremental construction and testing

Whatever approach you adopt, you have to decide whether implementation will proceed in stages, or until everything is completed. The former approach - building the system bit by bit - is known as *incremental design*, and is recommended. Although two modules may perform acceptably on their own, it's possible that problems will arise when they are made to operate side by side. By testing the skeleton system each time a new module is completed, problems can be identified early, and appropriate measures taken.

## Metaprogramming and fourth generation languages

*Metaprogramming* is a relatively recent approach to system implementation, introduced in [Lev87]. The idea is fairly straightforward, and operates under the same economic principles as the waterfall model itself. Implementation is a costly business, and can often be made cheaper with the use of purpose-built software tools. In many cases, therefore, development should actually begin with construction of development tools (*metaprograms*), rather than with direct coding of the product itself. Although this consumes additional resources in the early stages of implementation, the approach (it is claimed) more than makes up these losses during the later development stages. Levy estimates that roughly 80% of a major product can be generated by metaprogram, leaving the programmer free to develop the remaining more difficult (and more interesting) 20%. This approach carries an element of risk, however, since the development of the metaprogram is of no intrinsic worth to the customer - if *its* development runs over budget, the danger exists that you may end up with nothing to show the customer at all.

Where the application domain is fairly commonplace, metaprograms already exists, in the forms of *functional* and *fourth generation languages*. In both cases, we are able to specify what the result of a computation ought to be, without specifically stating how it is to be calculated. For example, in the domain of database management, for which most 4GLs have been designed, the user can make such queries as [Pre87,AIC86]

```
For the eastern and western regions,
how did actual sales for last month
compare with forecasts?
```

The use of advanced natural language interfaces, as in this example, coupled with fourth generation techniques, allows the user to apply his knowledge of the domain, free from the interference that would normally arise when forced to express his thoughts at low level in an artificial language.

In the same way, fourth generation languages have been developed in the form of *program constructors*, which allow the user to specify their needs at a very high level of abstraction. The program generator then converts the specification into a standard third generation language automatically. Unfortunately, most program generators are purely business oriented, and can only generate code in COBOL.

*Functional languages*, on the other hand, are ideal metaprograms for mathematical specifications, since some (e.g. HOPE+) are simultaneously specification *and* implementation languages. By writing your specification in such a language, no further translation is needed, since the specification itself is executable. Unfortunately, compilation of such specifications doesn't necessarily result in particularly efficient code.

The main advantage of metaprogramming techniques lies in the ease with which modifications can be made to the system. In general, faults and deficiencies within in the system, detected either during testing or after delivery, will be most easily expressed in terms of the original specification. By allowing modifications to be made at the level of the specification itself, metaprogramming avoids many of the problems of simple programmer error.


## Language considerations

Choosing an appropriate language is important, both because it effects the performance characteristics of the finished product, but also because language choice affects the way programmers think about problems. By thinking in terms of the 'wrong' language, you may inadvertently adopt an inappropriate design strategy. For example, if you are accustomed to using FORTRAN, you may ignore the possibility of using linked lists to simulate a stack structure, simply because this feature isn't directly supported by the language.

An implementation is more than just a working system. At some point, you can expect that the system will need maintaining. It is your responsibility to ensure that maintenance is as easy as possible. Similarly, your system should be easy to test. In addition to supplying the delivered system, therefore, implementation must also result in the production of intelligible documentation.


## Coding for maintenance

For maintenance purposes, the most direct source of information concerning a program is the code itself. There are several simple techniques which enhance the utility of this information.

The most direct technique is the use of suitable variable names. Some languages limit the number of characters that can occur in a variable name (e.g. BASIC), with the result that meanings can become obscured.

For example, a (badly written) package might include the following assignment statement

```
c := (f-32)*5/8
```

Unless you know the context in which this assignment is being made (which may not be clear simply from nearby program statements), it's impossible to know whether or not this statement is correct. A more thoughtful programmer might have written

```
centigrade_temp := (fahrenheit_temp-32)*5/8
```

from which it is evident that this statement has something to do with converting temperatures measured using the Fahrenheit scale into their equivalent centigrade value. A quick calculation, or a quick look in a reference book, soon shows that there is indeed an error (the '8' should be a '9').

A second feature of coding-for-maintenance is the appropriate use of *comments*. A common problem with commenting a program is knowing how many comments to include. This problem is reduced by sensible modular design. Comments should add information to the program, rather than simply paraphrasing the existing code, and as such can deal with the such features as

    * what is the intended use of this part of the code? what is it supposed to do?
      how is it invoked?

* what arguments does it assume, and what form must they take?

* where can I find more information about this algorithm or approach?

* how does this section of code relate to others?

* who wrote this? who audited it? when?

* has the code been modified at any time? why? in what way?

* what can go wrong? what precautions must I take when invoking this code?
  does it rely on the availability of any specific hardware or O/S features?

* has the author used programming features in a non-standard way?

By adopting a modular approach to system design, the code is naturally partitioned into 'information units'. Commenting can be used to address specific features in each module. For example, the following boxed information might be included at the head of a file in MSDOS.

Since all the code related specifically to the *Movedir* process has been collected in one place, it is sensible to incorporate details of usage and so on at the head of the module, where future maintainers of the file will most readily be able to relate it to the associated code. Comments of this kind which appear at the head of the module are called *prologue* comments. In addition, most code will require embedded *descriptive* comments, explaining what's going on in particularly tricky sections of the code, if doing so provides more clarity than including them elsewhere.

In all cases, comments should be accurate, should be clearly distinguished from the code itself, and should add information.

```
rem TITLE: movedir
rem
rem PURPOSE: to rename an existing directory
rem
rem MOTIVATION: a useful feature not directly supported
rem              in MSDOS
rem
rem USAGE: movedir current_name new_name
rem
rem ERROR MODES: MissPara (Missing_Parameters)
rem              NotValid (Specified path isn't valid)
rem              NotEmpty (Specified path already in use)
rem              SamePath (Specified paths are identical)
rem
rem WARNING: Current_name should be an existing, nonempty,
rem              directory.
rem          New_name should be a valid directory name,
rem              but should not yet be in use.
rem          Current_name and New_name should not be
rem              identical (usage error assumed).
rem
rem INVOKING MODULES: System, Tidy, TopShell
rem INVOKED MODULES:  Usage, FATedit
rem
rem AUTHOR: mps 12/7/90  AUDITED: sd 13/7/90
```

*Example 4.10*

## Coding for test

In addition to coding for maintenance, you are also coding for *testability*. Experience shows that, while many different systems can be designed that have the same intrinsic worth to the customer, some are easier to test than others. Once again, modular design can enhance the testability of a system, by allowing us to *locate* and *replace* the faulty module while leaving the rest of the system unaffected. In the case of fault-tolerant systems, it should be possible for the system to continue operating without interruption while a fault-free replacement is incorporated. Techniques for general and module testing are discussed at length in *Section 6.*

## Psychological factors

Some programmer errors are as much the fault of the language as of the programmer, and this should be taken into account when selecting your language. In general, all high-level programming languages are equivalent, in the sense that any one of them can be simulated in any other. However, this doesn't mean that they are all equally useful. For example, the following English phrases contain the same information.[7]

```
Version 1

Here's the corn the rat the cat the dog chased killed ate

Version 2

    The dog chased the cat
                  that killed the rat
                            that ate this corn
```

Most readers would agree, however, that *Version 2* is somewhat easier to understand. In the same way, just because two programs may have the same overall effect, it doesn't follow that they are just as easy to think about.

Besides specifically programmer-related issues of this kind, there are three language features which are believed to affect a programmer's performance [Pre87,Wei71].

---

[7] The implications of this example are considered at length in [Stannett M. *199? Theoretical issues in Software Engineering*. Chartwell-Bratt (to appear)].

**Ambiguity** affects all programmers. Although compilers are written in such a way that each statement should have only one possible 'meaning', it isn't always evident to the programmer or debugger what that meaning ought to be. For example, does "5/5*10" evaluate to 10 or 0.1? Indeed, this problem goes still deeper. In many cases, the original specification of the semantics of a language may be subtly ambiguous, resulting in code being treated differently by different compilers. Consequently, a statement may have different meanings depending on *where* it's being executed.

**Uniformity** is to do with such things as *consistency* and *overloadedness* in a language. For example, the symbol "+" is regularly used for integer-integer, integer-real and real-real addition, concatenation of strings, logical disjunction, specification of non-deterministic choice, and construction of datatypes. As the symbol becomes increasingly overloaded, the potential for programmer confusion increases also.

**Compactness** is related to the amount of information that has to be held in (human) memory in order to use the language. For example, one of the reasons why *Version 2* of the sentence above is easier to understand than *Version 1* is because its internal structure encourages logical 'chunking' of its content into meaningful sub-sentences.

### Problems inherent in implementation

No activity in software engineering is without its management problems. Yourdon [You82] notes four particular areas of concern.

**Testing** is often inadequate during the implementation stage. This is a particular problem where developers are working in a batch-processing environment (where jobs have to be submitted and run overnight, for example). Under such circumstances, debugging the product becomes increasingly tedious, and testing suffers accordingly.

**Hardware** may not be available for effective software construction. For a large system, you (or your company) will probably be recommending which hardware should be installed, as well as producing the software to run on it. Only the foolhardy would wait until the last minute before trying out their code on a new machine.

**Team working** has its own attendant difficulties, ranging from problems within teams (e.g. *I really can't stand that guy!*) to problems between teams (e.g. *Those b*****ds in finance won't give us the information we need!*), and this can lead to effective top-down design being impossible. Although each group develops its bit of the system top-down, the system as a whole is developed bottom-up.

**Mind reading** occurs when a programmer notices a gap in the specification, and attempts to fill it by guessing what was intended. It can lead to all sorts of problems, and should be avoided.

# Appendix

### Sociology : the growth of modularism

The lack of agreement as to what constitutes 'good design' is as prevalent in software engineering as elsewhere, partly because different designers attribute different weights to the various features which go to make up product quality. For example, Yourdon [You82] observes that many programmers and analysts regard a module as 'good' provided it makes efficient use of the available hardware.[8] In general, structured

---

[8] MPS: Given the ever decreasing costs of fairly reliable hardware, this view is increasingly mysterious. For example, the capabilities of my PC dwarf those of the mainframe I used ten years ago. It is estimated that a modern medium-range hand calculator now eclipses the computer systems used for the early Apollo missions - (footnote continues on next page).

design philosophies assume that good design is *cheap* design - hence today's emphasis on reducing excessive maintenance commitments.

In many ways this view has become outdated. The economic shockwaves initiated by the oil crises of the 1970s forced many industries to re-think the nature of management systems, until it is currently believed that something is 'good for the company' if it enhances its long-term strategic position [Por80]. Of course, the cheapest option is not necessarily the best under this criterion. In addition, this has to be coupled with the revolution in the nature of working practices and power relationships that has occurred since structured methods were first introduced.

As early as 1970, sociologists noticed that industrial society was no longer able to cope with the increasing speed of life which it had engendered, and new manifestations of this phenomenon are still reported [Han89]. The problem seems to lie at the very heart of top-down system design. Toffler [Tof70] gives the following example of the-way-things-were (and often still are). If a fault occurred in the mill at which he worked, it would be reported by the worker nearest the breakdown to his foreman. The foreman would then tell the production supervisor, who would notify the maintenance supervisor. Finally, the maintenance supervisor would send a crew to fix the problem. The astute reader will already have noticed, of course, that it would have been quicker, and somewhat cheaper, for the original worker simply to have fixed the problem himself, or else to have called the maintenance crew directly.

The crunch comes, of course, when the system is required to process inputs ever more quickly. Eventually, you cannot afford the luxury of sending messages up and down the hierarchy, simply because these communications are too time-consuming. Unfortunately, many of the 'structured' design methods in use today were first formulated when

---

Intriguingly, just as the PC market has become the predominant driving force in the development of computer technology, academia has become increasingly 'anti-PC', with many academics refusing to admit that they don't actually *need* highly expensive windowing systems - a PC would be just as good, at a fraction of the cost [Bar89].

monolithic bureaucracy was still regarded as the most efficient form of business organisation, an assumption embedded within the methods themselves.

As timeliness became increasingly bound up with business success, more and more instances of *sideways* communication became evident within successful companies, a process which was accelerated by the growth of high technology professions. Power began to shift from those at the 'top' of the organisation, to those whose judgements were based on such detailed specialisation that their supervisors were incapable of questioning them (including, thankfully, computer specialists!).

As individuals learned that personal success no longer relied on the success of the organisation for which they worked, so they became more mobile, and directed their allegiances in new directions. As conceptions of organisational structure changed, so did ideas as to the role of workers in business. For example, John Gardner, quoted in [Tov70], commented on the rise of 'professionalism',

> The loyalty of the professional man is to his profession and not to the organisation that may house him at any given moment ... even if he stays in one place his loyalty to the local organisation is rarely of the same quality as that of the true organisation man.

With only a few changes, this becomes a manifesto for modularism, since it states that, effectively, 'professional man' had arisen as the modular equivalent of 'organisational man':

> The affinity of the module is inherent in its functionality, and not in the particular system that may house it at any given moment ... even if it remains embedded in only one system, its affinity is rarely of the same quality as that of true monolithic code.

It appears that each generation's concept of 'good design' is heavily influenced by the predominant forms of social and political organisation which happen to be prevalent at the time. Undoubtedly, these organisations structures will undergo more (and more severe) convulsions as we approach and move into the next century. This opens up intriguing possibilities as to the future of design.[9]

---

[9] SD: A bye-product of the increasing interest in object-oriented programming is that software developers sell software implementations of such 'objects' as waste-paper bins, filing cabinets, etc., to be used by other developers in larger systems. Evidence of a more entrepreneurial generation of developer?

# Chapter 5

# Structure and Style

---

The structure of a computer system is an important
factor in its quality.  Obviously all systems, from a
huge project with two million lines of code to a small
ten line utility, have structure whether it is good or
bad.   It is the quality, strength and logic of the
structure that is important.

---

**Introduction**

'Structured design' and 'structured programming' have been buzz
phrases since the early seventies.  As with most overused phrases their
meaning has become unclear.  Some equate the absence of GOTO
statements as structured, others relate a particular diagraming technique
to structured development.  While both these factors can help in producing
quality software, the concept of structure as applied to design and
programming is more fundamental.

Structured design is the selection of program components which,
when connected in a specified way will solve a well specified problem.
Structured programming is a way of writing programs as a nested set of
single entry, single exit blocks of code using a restricted number of
constructs.

The consideration of the structure of both design and code together is relevant due to the increasing tendency to simplify or automate the transformation from design to code. The growing use of CASE tools, program generators and indeed inexperienced staff to produce code means that the majority of the structural decisions need to be made in the design phase.

This section will examine the objectives of the design process, the significance of modularity and some theoretical aspects of design and implementation. The section will end with a few 'rules of thumb' for modular systems and consideration of standards used in business.

**Design Objectives**

Designing software systems is a process of specifying a technical solution to a problem. The problem may be a business task such as payroll calculation or a technical requirement such as memory management in an operating system. The nature of the problem and the system requirements need to be established in the analysis phase. The structured approach to design and implementation involves producing the best solution to the problem.

In order to establish the best solution, objectives need to be stated upon which design decisions can be based. This is standard practice in all engineering disciplines. In strictly economic terms the lowest cost system that solves the complete problem is likely to be the best solution. This isn't to say that the cheapest system to develop will be the best, cost needs to be minimised over the entire life of the system.

Design goals, that when maximised, will contribute towards high quality systems are:

* **Efficiency.** The use of system resources such as processor time, storage, memory, peripherals and communications are the traditional items that are considered when system efficiency is to be enhanced. The reducing cost of hardware and increasing cost of staff has meant that the human factors of development, maintenance and testing need to be considered. If the purchase of extra memory will allow code to be written using a CASE tool rather that in a low level language, then the reduced development effort may justify the extra memory; however, if the increased execution time will require a processor upgrade, the equation may alter. The judgement of efficiency must account for all resources.

* **Reliability.** A common reliability measure for machinery is mean-time-between-failures (MTBF) ie. a washing machine may be expected to run trouble free for five years. In software, reliability must be part of the design. A washing machine will fail when a component wears out, a program will fail when an event causes incorrect code to execute. The code has not deteriorated over time, it was always wrong. The error may have only come to light because of a rare combination of data, but it was still an error. The design must validate data and cater for exceptions to avoid failures.

* **Maintainability.** A particularly important design goal is that when the system does go wrong it can be fixed accurately and quickly. The customer will be unhappy that the system has failed, taking a long time to develop a fix is only adding insult to injury. Figures for maintenance costs are often quoted as being 50% to 95% of an organisations systems budget. This shows how the cheapest to implement system may not be the lowest cost system when maintenance is accounted for. It is estimated that the average program fix introduces 1.7 errors. Systems designed with maintenance in mind must therefore reduce the overhead and dangers of maintenance.

* **Ease of modification.** Extending the goal of maintainability, systems generally are modified and enhanced throughout their life. The ease by which these modifications can be made obviously reduces the cost and increases the responsiveness of changes.

* **Flexibility.** The ease of applying the program or system to similar problems reduces the need for modifications. A pay-roll system designed to perform the monthly salary payments may be required to pay bonuses or collect social club subscriptions. A flexible system will be able to handle the adjusted input data thus avoiding the development and testing overhead of a modification.

* **Ease of use.** Ease of use is a requirement in the majority of systems, however it is often overlooked until implementation. The interface design and the input and output data need to be specified early in the design to ensure consistency. A technically brilliant system with an inconsistent interface will be used less than an average system with an intuitive, consistent interface.

* **Re-use.** A new project provides a valuable opportunity to create system components that can be used in later developments. The more maintainable, flexible and modifiable code is, the more likely it is to be re-used. The re-use of software is obviously very cost effective.

* **Simplicity.** Intelligence is of far greater value than 'cleverness' in systems development. The obscure code or design that is quite ingenious is often incomprehensible to others which does nothing for maintainability or modifiability.

Design should provide the best solution to the problem specified in the analysed requirements. The best solution will be the solution with the lowest cost for the life of the system. The life of the system will involve maintenance and is likely to involve modifications. Design and code need to maximise efficiency, reliability, maintainability, ease of modification, flexibility, ease of use, re-use and simplicity to achieve the lowest cost, best solution.

Simply providing a system is insufficient, designing and implementing the best solution within the time, cost and resource constraints is the only acceptable approach in professional systems engineering.

## Modularity

The structured approach to design can be summed up as 'Divide and Conquer' and 'Hide and Conquer'.  That is to say:

* The program / system should be made up of modular elements of code that each perform a specific function.

* The performance of a function and the data used should be hidden within the module.

Low cost, high quality, maintainable and easily modified systems are generally made up of parts that are:

* easily related to the problem (application)

* manageably small

* modifiable separately

This division of the problem into separate solvable units, then implementation of the system in corresponding small, separate parts is the principle of modularity.

In a modular system, each part of the system (module) corresponds to one small piece of the problem being solved, the relationships between modules corresponds to relationships between parts of the problem.

Modularity does not involve chopping a system into small parts arbitrarily. The size of a module does not itself determine the quality or maintainability of the system. Modules must relate to the problem domain and perform a single specific function to be effective.

A software module is analogous to a 'black box', only the inputs and outputs are visible to the rest of the system. The action of the 'box' can be exploited without knowing how it works, just what it does. The action of the 'box' has no effect on parts of the system other than the inputs and outputs.

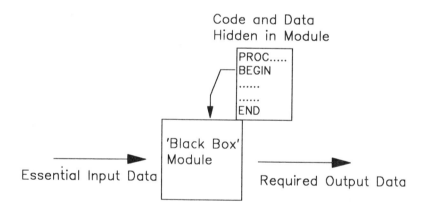

'Black Box' Modularity

*Figure 5.1*

Thus a module to open a file may:

    * accept inputs of a file name and an error flag

    * perform all the actions to open the file and check for errors

    * return an indication of success or error in the error flag

    * no other data items would be affected

Some modules will coordinate the performance of a number of functions by activating other modules. These control modules must still relate to an activity in the problem domain and should be of manageable size and perform a specific function.

These coordinating modules act like the management structure in a company, A regional sales manager coordinates the activities of local sales staff. The sales manager does not take responsibility for head office buildings or other unrelated tasks, but concentrates on optimising the performance of the local sales staff. Similarly a module that controls the calculation of pay-roll records would not initiate overnight back-up processing.

The production of modular systems can aid with maintenance, modification, testing and re-use by providing elements that are easily understood and that can be changed without dramatic side effects in other parts of the system. The extent to which a piece of code can be considered as a 'black box' is a reliable indication of the modularity of the code.

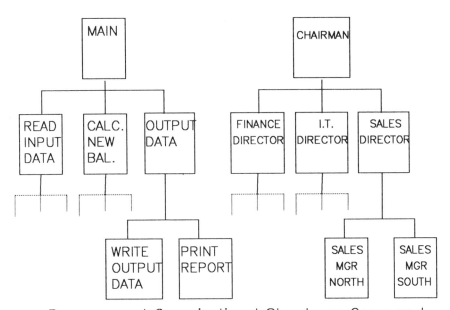

Program and Organisational Structures Compared

*Figure 5.2*

**Complexity**

Common sense tells us that the more simple a piece of code is the easier it is to:

    * get it right first time

    * fix it if it is wrong

    * change it to do something extra

Restricting design and code complexity is therefore a factor in producing quality systems.

Research into problem solving by psychologist George Miller [Mil56] identified that as the complexity of a problem increases the number of errors increases disproportionately. Miller found that people can mentally juggle around seven objects, entities or concepts at a time. The capacity for manipulating mental objects was found to be $7\pm2$, above which the number of errors increases significantly.

Miller's findings support the concept of modularity in that small, single function modules will generally manipulate small amounts of data, call a restricted number of other modules and have a small number of control constructs. The principle of performing a specific function is more relevant than module size. Splitting large monolithic code into 'modules' based on size alone will increase the complexity by introducing shared data between 'modules' and thus more objects to keep track of.

Complexity can be minimized in the module interface (or procedure / function call). The interface is less complex if the information is:

* presented locally - with the module call

* presented in a standard manner

* obvious

The call to an open file procedure OPENF(infile,errorflag) presents an obvious, standard interface with the information presented in the call (infile is clearly a file name and errorflag is a flag variable). A different module interface (call) such as OPENF(buffer[0]), where buffer contains a character count (n) in buffer[0] and the filename in buffer[1..n+1], the errorflag will be returned in buffer[0], is suitably opaque to illustrate how the interface can be made complex. Similarly if infile and errorflag have been set up in advance and OPENF is called without parameters, the interface is unclear.

Limiting the complexity of program modules and their interfaces is a major factor in producing quality software.

Two measures for assessing the complexity of a program or module are coupling and cohesion [YoC79,Bud89], these provide useful qualitative measures of structure.

## Coupling

The relationship between modules is important in assessing the complexity of a program. Modules that do not require any knowledge of any other modules are independent. Independent modules can be modified with minimal effect on the rest of the system. Modules that require knowledge of another module or modules are obviously dependent on those modules, changes to one may have an effect on the others. A module requiring knowledge of other modules is a form of connection between the modules. This connection of modules is represented by the concept of coupling.

Coupling is the degree of interdependence between modules. Highly coupled modules have a high dependence on each other, conversely loosely coupled modules are relatively independent. In general the higher the coupling between modules, the less like a 'black box' the module is, changes to one module is likely to have implications for the other. Minimising the coupling between modules reduces the system complexity proportionately.

Some factors that effect coupling in systems are:

* The type of connections between modules. Modules connected by parameters are more loosely coupled than those sharing global data.

* The complexity of the interface. Proportional to the number of items being passed between the modules ie. seven parameters represent higher coupling than two.

* The type of information flow along the connection. Data flow between modules represents lower coupling than control information flow.

* The binding time of the connection. Connections to identifiers assigned values at run time are more loosely coupled than connections to identifiers specified at coding. For example if a module has the processor type hard coded (ie. the processor type is specified at coding) the module is more tightly coupled to that data (more vulnerable to change) than if it used a system call to determine the processor type at run time.

Four major types of coupling that should be minimised during design and implementation are:

* **data coupling.** This is a measure of the data shared between modules, the parameters and shared external data. Obviously zero data coupling makes a module easy to modify and totally independent, unfortunately it would probably also imply that the module didn't do very much. To minimise data coupling, only the data actually needed by a module should be transferred to it. This essential data should be the only external data that the module uses. If a module needs to use one field of a complex record, only that one field should be passed to the module rather than the whole record. Global data or shared external data generally allows modules access to (and the ability to corrupt) unnecessary data and should therefore be avoided.

* **control coupling.** This is demonstrated by the use of a procedure
parameter as a 'switch' to determine how the procedure will function.


e.g.  PROCEDURE OPENF(Fname,mode;VAR err:int);
    BEGIN
      CASE mode OF
          "w" : {open for writing}
          "r" : {open for reading}
          "a" : {open to append}
            .

            .

            .

            .
      END;


The way in which the file is opened depends on the parameter 'mode', the flow of control of the procedure has been determined by an external dependence. This control coupling is often necessary, it may be clumsy to have procedures OPENF_WRITE, OPENF_READ etc. however the programmer needs to know the meaning of 'mode' and its action. This prevents the module from being a 'black box' and if used unwisely can considerably increase the complexity e.g. a module with two control parameters, each of which having three possible parameters can perform nine different tasks !

* **type (stamp) coupling.** This involves the sharing of a data type or definition (not the actual data), a change to the data type will have an impact on all the modules that use the definition. With a record data type that reflects the record structure in a database, the knowledge of the structure should be confined to the units that manipulate the record directly.

\* **common environment coupling.** In some languages a COMMON segment or common data area is created into which data shared by program segments is declared. Each item placed in such an area increases the coupling of all segments and modules since this shared data is available to all modules. The use of such data is sometimes necessary but must be used carefully since the action of any module using this common environment potentially effects every other module proportional to the number of common elements, hugely increasing complexity.

Coupling acts as a measure of the interdependence of modules. Working on the principle that reducing complexity improves software quality, the minimisation of the coupling of modules is desirable. It must be remembered that modules need to perform function and therefore communication between modules is necessary but only this necessary communication should connect modules.

**Cohesion**

Whilst coupling describes the relationship between modules cohesion measures the relationship of elements within a module. A module ideally is a 'black box' that performs a single function that relates directly to an aspect of the problem domain. The quality of a module depends on the functional relatedness of the statements to each other. Cohesion is a measure of the 'glue' that holds elements of a module together. If a module contains three elements X, Y and Z that each perform an action, the form of cohesion is a description of why X, Y and Z are together.

There are seven forms of cohesion exhibited by modules. In ascending order of desirability these are:

* **coincidental.** The elements are joined only by being in the same module. They are included on a random basis. This is fairly uncommon and generally results from 'chopping' a large piece of code into 'modules'. The function of such a module is unclear and therefore difficult to maintain.

* **logical.** The elements perform logically similar operations. For example a module that reads a character from a number of different sources e.g. keyboard, text file on tape, punched card, binary file on disk etc. While it is possible to see the rational behind this approach the amount of control information required by a logically cohesive module is large and the module will perform many different separate functions.

* **temporal.** The elements are concerned with operations performed at a particular time e.g. initialisation, end of day and restart routines. These elements are unlikely to perform functionally related tasks.

* **procedural.** Similar to temporal cohesion except that the elements are related by the order in which the operations are performed. This limits modification and re-use in that changing the sequence of actions requires changes to the module.

* **communicational.** Elements are concerned with the same input or output data. An example is a print module that accepts a number of data sources, assembles the line of a report and prints it. The dependence of the elements in the module on the input or output data provides a logical grouping.

* **sequential.** The outputs from one element in the module provides input data to the next processing element. Typical in procedures that perform an action 'then' another one e.g. read a record, convert the name to upper case, calculate the employees salary then print a pay-slip. As with communicational cohesion problems occur when one element is required independently.

* **functional.** All elements contribute to the execution of a single problem related task. It contains no extraneous elements. Classic examples are mathematical functions such as square root, logarithm etc. they perform a single problem related task.

Research into the cost of systems has shown that the first three types of cohesion (coincidental, logical and temporal) exhibit weak binding between elements of modules that suggests poor, costly design. The latter three types of cohesion (communicational, sequential and functional) contributed to efficient, reliable, maintainable systems.

An effective way of judging the cohesion of a module is to describe its function accurately in a single sentence. If the resulting sentence is simple with a single transitive verb and a specific non-plural object the module is likely to be functionally cohesive e.g. 'calculate the square root of the input number'. Other types of cohesion will require a compound sentence, a sentence with a comma or multiple verbs. Time oriented words such as 'first', 'next', 'after', 'then', 'until', 'for all' etc. suggest that the module probably has temporal, procedural or possibly sequential cohesion. Words such as 'initialise', 'house-keeping and 'clean-up' generally imply temporal cohesion. The absence of a single specific objective following the verb implies logical cohesion e.g. 'process all input records' or 'modify sales results'.

Cohesion is generally a retrospective measure of module quality. It can also be a useful indication of whether a processing element should be included in a module or not. The goal of functionally cohesive modules performing a single specific function should be sought after. Less cohesive modules are not however 'wrong' but may be able to be refined into more re-usable units. Strong cohesion and loose coupling should be used as indicators of design quality and to what extent modules can be further partitioned rather than laws that must be obeyed at all costs.

**Some ' Rules Of Thumb '**

Following on from some detailed measures of modularity and objectives for quality software this section presents some ideas that can be used to improve the structure of programs. They are not commandments or rules, rather they are checks or indicators that may be used to provide improvements in structure.

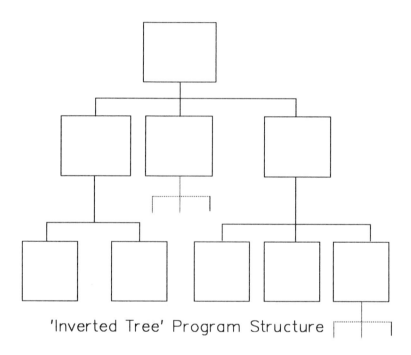

'Inverted Tree' Program Structure

*Figure 5.3*

**Program shape**

The shape of a program, will generally resemble an inverted tree. A master control module will call procedures at a lower level which will call further procedures.

The number of immediate subordinates of a module are referred to as the *fan-out* of the module. A module that directly calls six modules has a fan out of six. The size of fan out from a module can give an indication of design quality. A high fan-out, greater than $7\pm2$ (recall Millers findings) is generally of more concern than a low fan-out. High fan-out is often indicative of over active breakdown into modules or failure to identify intermediate levels in the design structure. The structure can be related to management structure, a manager with say 10 direct reports is unlikely to be effective in leading all ten.

Fan-in is, as you would guess, the inverse of fan-out. *Fan-in* is a measure of the number of modules that call a single module. Thus a standard module such as square route may be called by 8 modules and would therefore have a fan-in of eight. Fan-in is a desirable feature because each module with a fan-in greater than one is a re-use of code or a duplication of code avoided. Modules that exhibit functional cohesion are more likely to be widely used by other modules than those with sequence embedded. Structured design should lead to low level modules with a high fan-in. Fan-in should not be sought artificially by creating a large module with lots of uncohesive functions called by every other module. Where two modules perform similar functions there is generally scope for removing the common function to a module called from the original two modules.

In general a well designed system will exhibit higher fan-out in the high level modules (as lower modules are selected and controlled) and higher fan-in in the lower level modules (as the basic functions are implemented). This produces a graphical structure of the modules which is 'mitre' shaped. This 'shape' of a system is not a design tool but a clue to the soundness of the structure.

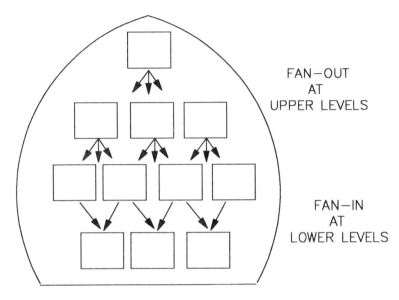

'Mitre' Shaped Program Structure

*Figure 5.4*

**Program depth**

The depth of the system is the number of levels in the module hierarchy. This provides a clue to the size and complexity of the system. The depth needs to be logical. If the system consists of one hundred lines of code and has a depth of twelve this could be the sign of over enthusiastic division of code into modules. Similarly if the system has one million lines and a depth of three, there could well be scope for subdividing some of the modules.

## Data flow in modules

Some basic categories of modules can be identified in terms of data flow:

* **Afferent flow.** Data is passed to a module from a subordinate module, possibly transformed within the module and then passed to a superordinate module. For example a module to add interest to an account balance uses the value returned from a interest calculation module, adds it to the account balance and then returns the new balance to the calling module.

* **Efferent flow.** Data is passed to a module from a superordinate module, possibly transformed within the module and then passed to a subordinate module. An example is a print formatting routine that receives a data record, formats it and then passes the formatted data to a print module for printing.

* **Transform flow.** Data passed to a module by a superordinate module, transformed and then returned to the superordinate e.g. a call to a module that calculates interest.

* **Coordinate flow.** Data received from a subordinate module is passed, possibly altered, to another subordinate module. For example a module that updates an account balance calls a 'read record' module and if a record is read successfully calls a 'calculate new balance' module passing it the balance and transaction data from the record.

Modules that exhibit afferent flow can be termed afferent modules, similarly efferent modules etc.

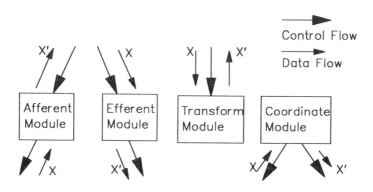

Modules Categorized By Data Flow

*Figure 5.5*

This categorisation of modules can be useful in deciding whether a module is doing the right job, in the right place, at the right time. A general model of systems shows that:

* modules at the lowest level are likely to be transform modules

* modules concerned with the input of data are likely to be afferent

* modules concerned with output are likely to be efferent

* coordinate modules will exist high in the hierarchy

* the data manipulation routines are likely to be mainly transform modules.

This leads to a 'Transform-centred' structure that has been found to be common amongst low cost reliable systems.

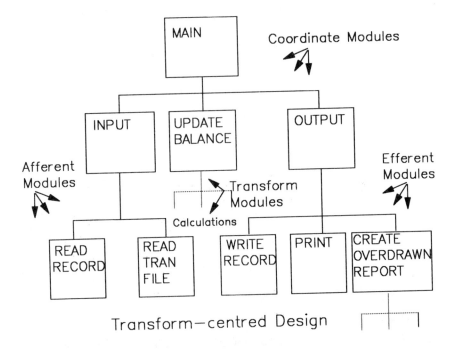

Figure 5.6

## Module size

The size of a module (number of lines or statements) is perhaps the most dangerous 'rule of thumb' to present. A statement that 'x lines is the ideal module size' can be blindly adhered to quite easily with the effect that a logical module that consists of 5x lines of code is split into 5 tightly coupled illogical modules or that three small functionally cohesive modules are combined to get the line count up to the magic x, making a coincidentially associated procedure.

The size of a module is significant with regards to its maintainability and modifiability, if it is of manageable size it is more likely to be easy to understand and to fix or change. There are many ideas on module size, popular line count figures are in the range 24 (lines on a standard VDU) to 60 (lines on a page of printer paper).

The shorter a module the easier it is to understand but this should never assume greater importance than the need to perform a functionally cohesive task. If the only way to perform a single function is with a 500 line module, that is the ideal size, similarly if three line do the job as in some mathematical functions, that is the right size.

## Use of literals and constants

As mentioned previously, the later in the processing that an identifier is assigned a value, the easier it is to modify. If a module that produces printer output is written to output 80 column lines, with the literal 80 in the code (and possibly checks for column 75, 81 etc.) the modification for a printer with 132 columns will be more difficult than if a constant 'printer_max_columns' were used. If the maximum columns the printer could support where part of a printer definition data table, read at run time, the printer could be changed without any code modification. In general literal values are difficult to modify, constants are easier but require recompilation and data read at run time provides the most flexibility.


## Global data variables

The earlier description of coupling has probably shown that global data variables increase complexity and the danger of modules having side effects (altering things that have nothing to do with their function). Few programs will have no global data, but the use of such data should be limited to where strictly needed. Data items such as buffers, loop variables etc. that are frequently treated as 'dogsbody' items that can be used for any purpose in any module are a major cause of errors and should not be used. The processor and memory overhead of declaring a local buffer or loop variable is in general amply compensated by increased reliability and ease of maintenance.

When the use of global variables is minimised, the only way of transferring data to modules is as parameters. When passing parameters it is essential that only the data needed by the module is passed. If you don't pass extra data to a procedure it can't be inadvertently corrupted and the interface to the procedure is generally simpler.


## House  Styles  and  Coding  Procedures

Software houses and IT development areas in large organisations generally establish local guide-lines to cover analysis, design and implementation. These 'house styles' or procedures are an attempt to achieve consistency throughout the organisation.

Interface standards are the most common form of in house guide-lines. The display of error messages, the structure of menus, use of colour, inverse video etc. are standardised to present a common applications interface. Such standards are essential and are generally supported with library procedures to handle screen output. IBM have issued Common User Access guide-lines (CUA) in an attempt to set an interface standard throughout the industry and across all hardware platforms, there are separate CUA standards for text and graphical user interfaces.

Other standards often specify such things as:

* the design method and tools to be used.

* security standards.

* necessary documentation

* restrictions in the use of constructs e.g. no GOTO statements.

* layout e.g. the information in module headings, indentation in loops, conditional statements etc.

* the use of comments. Views on comments varies widely, clear code is not made clearer by the use of comments, bad code is only explained by comments, it is not improved.

* naming conventions covering the names of variable, constants, procedures, functions, library procedures etc.

In house standards vary in size and quality from organisation to organisation. Some are based on sound software engineering techniques, some may be left over from a bygone era, with poor practices recommended in the name of efficiency and some don't exist at all.

The existence of such local styles and standards does not make them correct or timeless. To be effective they should be regularly updated to reflect modern software engineering methods and techniques. Most importantly they should help rather than hinder the achievement of high quality, low cost software.

# Chapter 6

# Testing

## The commercial relevance of testing

> The goal of any business activity is to enhance long-
> term competitive position. Testing is expensive. No
> sensible company should condone this expense unless
> clear strategic benefits can be obtained.[1] Rather than
> produce yet another `guide to testing', of which many
> are already available on the market, we have tried to
> concentrate instead on the underlying issues involved.

The goal of any business activity is to enhance long-term competitive position, and it is in this light that we examine *software testing* during this course, especially as it relates to modular design. If testing is to be seen as a purely commercial activity, it follows that (besides being impossible) testing a product until you are certain of its functionality is undesirable. Testing is expensive, and suffers from the usual problems of diminishing returns.

> A basic principle of managerial economics is that one should continue
> a given activity so long as the benefit to be derived from the last unit
> of activity exceeds the cost of that unit of activity [Lev87].

---

[1] This section is contracted and adapted from [Stannett M. 1990 *Software Testing*. (Short course lecture notes)].

In other words, as soon as the benefits to be gained from further testing are outweighed by the costs of performing these tests, you should stop. This principle is widely adopted. For example, a supplier might release their products onto the market when the estimated costs of further testing become equal to the expected costs of maintaining the product.

Adopting this policy raises a major problem: how do we estimate the relative costs of further testing, as opposed to product release? On the one hand, it is well-known that testing a product can never demonstrate its correctness conclusively.[2] Consequently, we can never know exactly how many faults remain embedded in the product when we release it onto the market, nor how expensive they are likely to prove. On the other hand, it isn't entirely certain how to determine the costs of testing itself. In many instances, it is difficult, if not impossible, to separate *testing* from the distinct but related activity of *debugging*. Unfortunately, debugging is notoriously imprecise, and can cause more problems than it solves. Indeed, not even formal mathematical methods are exempt from the problems of human error, as we observed in *Chapter 4*.

There are five major forces which affect the competitive position of a software company.

* Competitors

   This is the most obvious form of competitive pressure you will face, namely the active competition of other companies within the industry, or departments within your own company. It's possible to force competitors to leave an industry, but only if *exit barriers* are sufficiently low. For example, offering to take over maintenance contracts from a competitor may make it easier for them to divest their software interests.

* Suppliers

   In many instances, your suppliers can exercise a great deal of control over your activities. For example, if you have committed yourself to IBM

---

[2] In any case, this isn't what testing is about.

hardware products, this may limit the range of software tools available to you.

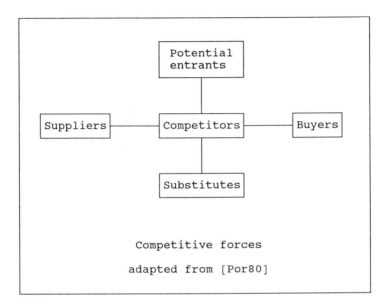

*Figure 6.1*

* Buyers

    Some customers can have such great buying power that their decisions will have a effect upon your own. For example, companies which traditionally sell to the Ministry of Defence have no option but to implement Ministry policies (e.g. 00-55) if they want to retain their business.

* New entrants

    There is always a risk that new companies may enter the industry, and so become competitors. This risk is higher whenever *entry barriers* are low. This occurs when the costs involved in setting up in the industry are relatively low.

* Substitutes

> There is always the risk that new technology may emerge which renders your own product obsolete. For example, in the early days of computing, when only mainframes were available, it was possible to send work to computer service bureaux. As minicomputers, and eventually PCs, became available, so companies were able to afford the costs involved in carrying out this work themselves.

## Topic for discussion / argument

> We suggest that a sensible testing strategy can reduce the pressure exerted by at least three of these major forces. Consequently, testing can be seen as central to maintaining and enhancing strategic position within the software industry.

## Testing and competitors

Essentially, there is only one way to outperform your competitors - offer your target market a better product. It's essential to remember, however, that a product is more than just the delivered software. Traditionally, the *marketing mix* for a given product comprises four features.

### Product

> What does the product actually do for the customer? Is it hardware, software, maintenance, or some other service? Is the product of sufficient *quality* to warrant its cost?

### Distribution

> How easily can potential customers acquire your product? For example, on-site maintenance entails a wide distribution network (essentially, each customer is an outlet), and customers are prepared to pay a premium for

this service, compared with narrow distribution return-to-base services. (For example, Viglen will supply on-site maintenance on a basic colour model PC$^3$ for approximately 8% of the original product price).

### Price

In general, making a product more expensive will encourage customers to shop elsewhere.[4] Once your price is fixed, however, all other costs must be recouped from the associated income. Choosing the correct price requires you to take these contradictory factors into account. One point is clear, however. Reducing your own costs can only be beneficial, provided quality is unaffected, since it gives you more flexibility in setting your product price.

### Promotion

Promotion takes many forms, but it is generally true that the most effective form of promotion is free, namely word-of-mouth recommendation from satisfied customers.

Testing contributes favourably to all four elements of the marketing mix for software products. Appropriate testing contributes to product quality, and so aids you in the battle with your established competitors. If you offer maintenance services, testing can reduce your distribution costs (if a customer encounters fewer faults, it will cost you less to service that outlet). By reducing maintenance costs, production costs can be reduced significantly, thus enhancing your price flexibility (maintenance generates a significant proportion of total product cost).[5] Finally, more customers are likely to recommend your product if it breaks down less often.

---

[3] A recently acquired VIG I+, with 40 Mb hard disk, 1 Mb RAM, 1.44 Mb high-density floppy, keyboard, mouse, and VGA colour monitor cost roughly £1530 (inc. VAT @ 15%), while on-site maintenance for the same system costs approx. £126 for one year (inc. VAT). All prices as at May 1990.

[4] However, making a product too cheap will encourage some potential customers to regard your product as being of low quality.

[5] "... the data on software maintenance expenditures can only be called *horrifying*; figures range from a low of 50% to as high as 80-90%." [Lev87]

## Testing and new entrants

Testing works indirectly to deter new entrants by raising entry
barriers. Because appropriate testing reduces your maintenance costs,
more resources are free for investment in other aspects of production, e.g.
research and development. Consequently, new entrants have not only to
match your reduced costs, but also your enhanced production.

## Testing and buyers

Very few buyers are unaccountable. Consequently, it is in their
interests to opt for the product offering the highest quality at the lowest
cost. Testing can help to ensure that this product is your own.

## Documentation   and   Testing

Traditionally, testing is carried out as part of the process of ensuring
product quality. However, as we observed during our discussion of formal
design techniques in *Section 4*, there are many aspects to product quality.
Unlike formal design, software testing deals almost all of these aspects.
However, we shall concentrate on testing as it relates to the code itself,
rather than its relationships to the user and the system in which it is
embedded.

Of the neglected aspects, two of the most important are *readability*
and *maintainability*, both of which can be summed up in the question '*is
your documentation adequate?*' As far as possible, software should be self-
documenting, but there will always be a need for additional material. In
particular, the information supplied to the user should be complete. Laski
[Las89] notes that two systems may satisfy the same specification, and yet
produce different outputs for the same input. He continues,

> In one case, a programmer, whose program produced a correct solution different from [the example] given in the specification, spent a considerable time 'debugging' the program!

This example demonstrates that a system may be reliable, in the sense that it satisfies its specification, and yet may be considered by the user to be faulty, because either the interface or the instructions which come with the product are insufficiently clear. Unfortunately, good documentation as a matter of course seems a long way off. Levy's comment bears repeating:

> One important area in which I do not see any progress is in the productivity or quality of documentation. Documentation is a significant part of software, but I see no hopeful signs ... it will require much research to achieve significant results in this area [Lev87].

## The continuing need for software testing

Modern theoretical methods allow us to produce provably correct programs, in the sense that they do precisely what their specifications tell them to, and nothing else. However, the formal approach to program derivation doesn't remove the need for careful testing of the finished product. There are a number of reasons, some of which we touched upon in *Section 4*.

**Incorrect specifications.** Formal design methods require that the initial specification should be unambiguously expressed in the form of a mathematical statement about the program's required functionality. Unfortunately, the translation of customer requirements into mathematical format is a difficult process, requiring a great deal of skill and patience. In general, the customer won't understand the language in which the specification is eventually written, while its author may have only a passing knowledge of the customer's business environment.

Consequently, while the program may match its specification exactly, it is highly probable that the specification itself will fail to represent the customer's requirements correctly. In addition, the customer's requirements are likely to change with time, so that the specification will need periodic maintenance. Testing is required to decide whether and where the specification is inadequate.

**Side effects from other programs.** Formal proofs of program correctness assume that the program is protected from outside interference. In a concurrent or time-sharing environment, programs may interact with each other in unexpected ways, e.g. by overwriting shared areas of system memory.

**Hardware considerations.** There is as yet no known method for establishing the correctness of the hardware platform on which the program will run. Although a program may be correct, it could still produce erroneous output if it is intolerant of hardware faults.

### Module   testing

Because testing is such a difficult process, it makes sense to break the testing activity up as much as possible. Testing a program module by module has three advantages. First, it makes it somewhat easier to locate the error, since we already know the module in which it is to be found. Second, a module is likely to require fewer testcases than the program as a whole, because it is smaller. Third, testing can be carried out on several sections of the code simultaneously.

As always, the aim of module testing is to show that the module does *not* satisfy its specification; consequently, we must have available both the source code, *and* its specification. It is easier to satisfy this requirement if the design process was itself modular, since the specification will already have been broken into functional units.

Module testing is only one stage in the full testing process. Once each module has been tested, and considered satisfactory, it is necessary to join them together as laid down by the program structure. At this point, testing has to recommence on the program as a whole, to ensure that no errors have arisen due to the integration process itself. And finally, of course, the system as a whole must be tested once the program has been embedded within it.

The techniques available for module testing are the same as for programs in general.

## Styles of testing

In general, there are four approaches available for testing. Three of these, *black-box*, *white-box*, and *mixed* (we call this mixture of black-box and white-box testing *"dual-view"*) are standard techniques with a long pedigree. A fourth strategy, *dual construction*, is currently undergoing development and evaluation as part of a joint research project between members of the Formal Methods Research Group in our own department, and members of the Electronics Department at Hull University.

In all four cases, we study the system specification carefully in order to determine which inputs are particularly 'sensitive', in the sense that if an error is present in the system, it will cause the wrong output to be produced for at least one of these inputs. In addition, there is a fifth approach to software testing, *design-for-testability*, closely related to dual-construction.

## White-box testing

In the case of white-box testing, we base our choice of test-cases upon the internal structure of the program. Notice that it isn't enough just to look at the individual program statements: we also need to consider how these statements are 'stuck together'. Failing to make this simple observation leads many novices to suggest that an adequate means of testing a program is to supply enough test cases to ensure that each statement is executed at least once.

## Black-box testing

As commercial systems increase in size, so their control structures are becoming too complex to test adequately using white-box testing techniques. Black-box testing concentrates entirely upon the system specification, and tests the *functionality* of the program. Because black-box testing techniques make no assumption about the actual structure of the program in question, they can be used to generate test strategies *before* program design has commenced. This is of particular importance in *dual construction*.

## Design-for-testability

Design-for-testability (DFT) is an important consideration in hardware production, and one which we expect to grow in importance for software. Experience shows that while many different programs may be written which perform the same task, some will be inherently easier to test than others. By identifying those design styles which facilitate system testing, we essentially elevate *testing* from its role as an 'after-thought' within the traditional *software life cycle* to a position of primary importance.

## Dual construction

*Dual construction* arises from an attempt to formalise functional testing of high integrity VLSI, as part of the DTI/IED *Silicon towards 2000* project. Although our initial emphasis is on hardware, the approach carries over in full to software. The aim of our project is as simple as it is ambitious:

> Given a specification of a function to be implemented in silicon, construct a testing strategy for the chip on which it will be implemented.

This is particularly non-trivial, because we have to engineer a test-strategy for a chip which doesn't yet exist, and most likely won't be designed until some time later. Unfortunately, it's been long established that it's theoretically impossible to design a system which can verify the functionality of randomly presented systems (where 'systems' can be either hardware or software). Consequently, we are forced to take control of the production process itself.

*Dual construction* refers to the construction of *two* strategies simultaneously - one for the design of the system, the other for its testing - each influencing the other. In effect, *dual construction* is a form of incremental DFT. The project is nearing the end of its first year, and the work has not progressed sufficiently for judgements to be made about its eventual viability.

## The logistics of testing

It is often stated that testing is carried out to ensure that a system is working properly. This is wrong. Testing is always destructive. Except in the most exceptional cases, a commercial software product will necessarily

contain errors. The role of testing is to *expose* these errors, so that they can
be corrected.

Myers [Mye79] suggests the following guidelines for improving your
chances of detecting errors in a piece of software.

* Don't forget to specify the correct outcome  of your test.

* Never test your own software.

* Inspect the results of each test thoroughly.

* It's not enough to test whether the software does what it should. You
  should also check that it doesn't do what it shouldn't.

* Never use throw-away test cases.

Although these guidelines all represent common sense, they are often
forgotten. Let's examine them in more detail.

* If an error is particularly subtle, or is embedded deep within the software,
  it is possible that the output produced for a given input is only slightly
  different from its 'correct' value. Unless the latter is clearly documented,
  and the output from the test is thoroughly checked, it is likely that the
  tester may fail to notice that an error has occurred.

* This problem is underlined if a programmer or an organisation is
  responsible for testing its own products. In some cases, a programmer
  may fail to notice the most glaring of errors - people tend to see what
  they *think* is there, rather than what actually is.

* In general, users of a program will be unaware of its limitations, and may
  attempt to use it in circumstances not intended by its designer. Testing
  should take place to determine that incorrect usage of the program does

not lead to erroneous, but apparently meaningful, output being produced.

* Test-cases are a valuable product, and it is not cost-effective to 're-invent' the same test-case several times over for the same program. Unfortunately, this frequently happens when programmers invent test-cases and patch up errors 'on the fly'.

## Walkthroughs and inspections

With the exception of *dual construction,* which is still under development, each style of testing has various techniques with which it is associated. White-box testing assumes that you have the code available for inspection, and can take one of two forms, depending upon whether the principle agent of testing is human or machine. For the purposes of this course, we shall consider a few techniques for white-box testing, but you may like to consult the literature for further details of other techniques.

Traditionally, it was believed that the only use to which code should be put was the control of a computer. However, largely in response to Weinberg's book *The psychology of computer programming* [Wei71], a view emerged during the 1970s that code should also be read by humans, and that this would provide a useful testing platform. Two principal forms of human-based testing are *walkthroughs* and *inspections.* These are both so straightforward that they seem, at first sight, pointless. However, human-based techniques have proven fairly successful. In both cases, it is essential that the participants treat the meeting constructively. If the programmer is made to feel threatened, the techniques become largely ineffective. Rather than regarding a programmer as 'lousy' because they've made mistakes, the team should appreciate that errors occur as an intrinsic part of the programming process itself. Indeed, the restraint required of the programmer, for the techniques to be fully effective, is a test of character in itself. If the session reveals a large number of errors, or a few errors of especial significance, it may be necessary to convene a repeat session after the corrections have been implemented.

**Walkthroughs.** Code walkthroughs involve a team of between three and five committed individuals, examining the a piece of code in depth. Each session lasts between 1½ and 2 hours. Three of the team members have special roles: moderator, secretary, and tester, and one member of the team (who shouldn't be the moderator) is the author of the code.

The *moderator* co-ordinates the session, making sure that copies of all relevant documents and other materials are circulated to team members in plenty of time. During the session, the moderator also ensures that team members participate constructively. The *secretary* keeps notes of all the errors discovered during the session - these will be required later by the programmer. Finally, the *tester* comes prepared with a small number of test cases. The actual nature of these cases isn't very important - their significance lies in initiating a question and answer session between the programmer and the other team members.

During the session, the test cases are tried out one by one, with all computations being carried out by the team members themselves. It's usual to keep a record of the on-going state of the program during the walkthrough on a blackboard or paper, to make it easy to keep track of what's going on. In the context of this course, we regard paper records of walkthroughs as important deliverables, and require you to submit them as part of your project.

If difficulties arise, team members are encouraged to ask the programmer precisely what's going on in the relevant part of the program (frequently, the programmer may notice a mistake before any of the others).

**Inspections.** Inspections are similar to walkthroughs, in that the group size and session length are much the same. This time, we only have one special role, that of moderator. As before, the moderator keeps everything running smoothly, and should be someone other than the programmer. Although the moderator is expected to be proficient at programming, they don't require any particular familiarity with the program under discussion.

During the meeting, the programmer talks the team through the program, one statement at a time, explaining the logic behind the various algorithms as he or she does so. From time to time, team members may have difficulty following the argument, and are encouraged to ask for clarification. In general, a session will cover around 250 lines of code, so that substantially longer programs have to be dealt with in multiple sessions (simply extending the length of a single session doesn't work, because the participants become mentally exhausted, and unable to participate effectively).

**Evaluation.** Technically, the aim of both walkthroughs and inspections is to detect errors, and is *not* debugging. However, there is some evidence to suggest that actively trying to debug a program during the session can encourage the detection of deeply embedded logical flaws [Fre75], if it allows team members to investigate the underlying semantics of the program. Practical experience shows that the techniques are effective, with between 30% and 70% of all errors which are eventually discovered being discovered using human-based methods [Mye78] (IBM claim 80% effectiveness [Per77]).

### Computer-based techniques

Besides simply reading through the code, it's possible actually to run the program. For this to be worthwhile, however, we need to be sure that the inputs (or *test cases*) we select have a high probability of showing up the presence of errors. In particular, if we try lots of different inputs, one at a time, we should try to ensure that their collective chances of showing up errors are as high as possible.

One technique would be to try enough test cases to ensure that every statement of the program is executed at least once. This is certainly necessary, but is nowhere near sufficient, because it doesn't ensure that the statements are actually 'put together' properly. For example, consider the following very simple PASCAL-like program.

```
PROGRAM quench;

TYPE object = ...;

CONST full = 500;
      safe_minimum = 100;

VAR kettle_contents : INTEGER;
    thirsty : BOOLEAN
    kettle  : object
    coffee  : object


PROCEDURE boil (kettle : object)
{boil water in kettle}
END;

PROCEDURE make (coffee : object)
{add water to cup with coffee}
END;


BEGIN
kettle_contents := full;
WHILE kettle_contents > safe_minimum
DO BEGIN
    input(thirsty);
    IF thirsty
    THEN BEGIN
        boil(kettle);
        make(coffee)
        END;
    END;
END.
```

*Example 6.2*

Technically, this program has only *two* statements, and a single test case is all that is required. Clearly, this isn't sufficient, since this won't allow us to check out all the different ways in which the statements might be executed. By regarding the program as comprising three modules (*boil, make,* and the program body itself) we can generate a slightly better test set, but not much better.

A more sensible approach would be to insist that every possible path through the program should be exercised. That is, we draw a flow-chart of the program, work out every path through the chart, and devise a test case for each such path. This is, however, not always possible, since

* there may be an infinite number of paths through the chart;

* not all the paths may be realisable in practice; this may be inherent in the problem being solved by the program, or it may be due to a coding or logical error of some kind.

It is clear, however, that such a test would have more chance of spotting errors than simply executing each statement once. Unfortunately, it is still possible that errors may be missed. It may happen that two distinct choices of test case will cause the various decisions in a program to be resolved differently, but that the *combinations* of decisions conspire to cause the same path to be traversed. For example, in the following section of flow-chart (*Chart 6.3*), all three of the boxed resolutions (*Box 6.4*) lead to traversal of the 'No' path.

Clearly, we need to ensure not only that all *paths* are traversed, but also that all *decisions* are enacted.

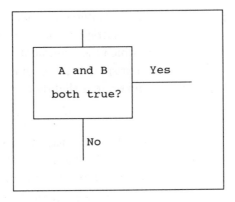

*Chart 6.3*

```
A = false     B = true
A = true      B = false
A = false     B = false
```

*Box 6.4*

It is worth pointing out, however, that even such full coverage as this cannot guarantee the correctness of the code. For example, the program *quench* has a fatal flaw which would not be picked up without thorough analysis of the specification, and common-sense. At no point in the program are the contents of the variable *kettle_contents* decreased (so that one of the decisions we would like to enact is physically unrealisable for the *wrong* reasons), so that using this program to control an automatic coffee-maker would probably result in damage to the element.

# Appendix

### System testing

There are at least 15 types of system testing that should be carried out once the program has been judged suitable for use [Mye79], and it is not possible for us to consider these in appropriate depth in the week allowed for this course. For reference purposes, we list the various types here. Further details may be found in the literature.

* *configuration testing* (what happens to the program when we change the system configuration?)

* *conversion testing* (can we upgrade the program easily in the future? is it compatible with other programs we might want to use?)

* *documentation testing* (can you understand it? is it useful?)

* *facility testing* (has everything been remembered?)

* *installability testing* (is the program easy to install?)

* *performance testing* (are response times low enough, and throughput rates high enough?)

* *procedure testing* (does it fit appropriately into the 'larger' systems of the company?)

* *recovery testing* (is it easy to restart the system after a crash?)

* *reliability testing* (is the down-time per year low enough? how many unique errors are allowed to occur after installation?)

* *security testing* (would hackers find it a pushover?)

* *serviceability testing* (how easily can we maintain the system?)

* *storage testing* (is there enough storage available, of the right type?)

* *stress testing* (what happens when the volume of data increases substantially over a short period of time?)

* *usability testing* (how good is the interface?)

* *volume testing* (what happens when we increase the volume of data with which the system has to cope?)

# Appendix A

# A Typical Project

---

In addition to attending course lectures, students
are required to carry out a concurrent one-week team
project. The ideal team size seems to require four
individuals working co-operatively. At the end of the
week, each group has to demonstrate its system (all
members must be present). Then comes the acid test: a
change to the original specification is announced,
and the teams have 30 minutes in which to draw up a
schedule of the detailed changes that will be
required of their design. In the nature of
interactive projects, the description given here is
only a starting point - assessors and students will
develop their own refinements as the week progresses.

---

### The required system

A school runs a savings bank. The local branch of a major high
street bank provide the school with bank books, deposit facilities, and
promotional free gifts. Naturally, because of the high quality promotional
gifts, the paper-work involved in maintaining ledgers, giving balances and
statements, etc., is imposing too heavy a burden upon the hard-worked
staff and students who administer the bank.

A computer system, as proposed by Form 2a, is required. They
suggest that it should do the following.

* be rugged and sturdy, because of the heavy demands placed upon them
  during the banking sessions

* run on an IBM compatible machine, because that's what they've got in the school already

* be 'user-friendly', i.e. the staff should be able to understand it as well.

The accounts are deposit accounts with the prevailing annual interest rate (currently 9%). Interest accrued is calculated each Monday, and added to the accounts. The relationship the school has with the students is identical to the relationship the bank has with the school. Banking sessions are held only on Tuesdays.

If any depositor wishes to withdraw their money, they must give at least one week's notice. The minimum sum that can be withdrawn at any one time is £5 (or their balance, if this is lower). A report is needed of the intended withdrawals for the following week, so that the money can be ordered from the high street bank.

Depositors should be able to find out their current balance at the Tuesday banking sessions. Obviously a record of payments made, and the accounts to be credited, needs to be produced at the end of business each Tuesday.

### Project deliverables

* work plans, milestones, etc.
* design documentation
* program specifications
* test plans
* minutes of walkthroughs
* program listings
* a working system

The adage *quality rather than quantity* applies to documentation. Your work will be marked accordingly. Marks will be awarded for the project team as a whole, not to individuals. If a team decides that any of its members are not pulling their weight, they should notify the assessors who will adjust the scores accordingly.

# Bibliography

[AIC86]   *Intellect System Documentation* 1986 Artificial Intelligence Corporation, Waltham, MA, USA.

[Ale71]   Alexander C. 1971 *Notes on the Synthesis of Form*. Harvard University Press.

[BiB88]   Bittanti S. and Bolzern P. 1988 *An introduction to software reliability modelling*. In [Bit88], pp 1-42.

[Bit88]   Bittanti S. (*ed.*) 1988 *Software reliability modelling and identification*. LNCS **341**. Springer.

[Boo86]   Booch G. 1986 *Object-oriented development*. IEEE Trans. on Software Engineering, SE-12, 211-21.

[Bro75]   Brooks F. 1975 *The Mythical Man-Month* Addison Wesley.

[Bud89]   Budgen D. 1989 *Software Development with Modula-2* Addison Wesley.

[Cut87]   Cutts G. 1987 *SSADM, Structured systems analysis and design methodology*. Paradigm Press.

[Dai78]   Daily E.B. 1978 *Software development*. Proc. European Computing Review, Infotech International.

[Dat81]   Date C.J. 1981 *An Introduction to Database Systems*. Addison Wesley.

[DaW89]   Daniels J. and Wallace C. 1989 *'Object-Oriented Design' Course Notes*. IIR Technology.

[DCC88]   Downs E., Clare P. and Coe I. 1988 *SSADM application and context*. Prentice Hall.

[Deu82]   Deutsch M.S. 1982 *Software verification and validation: realistic project approaches*. Prentice-Hall.

[DeM78]   DeMarco T. 1978 *Structured Analysis and System Specification*. Yourdon Press.

[DeM87]   DeMarco T. 1987 *Controlling Software Projects*. Yourdon Press.

[DMM87]    DeMILLO R.A., McCRACKEN W.M., MARTIN R.J. and PASSAFIUME J.F. 1987 *Software testing and evaluation*. Benjamin/Cummings.

[Dro89]    DROMEY G. 1989 *Program derivation - the development of programs from specifications*. Addison-Wesley International.

[DuN81]    DURAN J.W. and NTAFOS S. 1981 *A report on random testing*. Proc 5th Int.Conf.S.E., March 9-12, 1981, San Diego, CA, pp 179-83.

[Fag76]    FAGAN M.E. 1976 *Design and code inspections to reduce errors in program development*. IBM Systems J. **15**(3) pp 182-211.

[Fai85]    FAIRLEY R.E. 1985 *Software engineering concepts*. McGraw-Hill International.

[Fre75]    FREEMAN R.D. 1975 'An experiment in software development'. *The Bell Systems Technical J., Special Safeguard Supplement*, S199-S209.

[GMP88]    GHEZZI C., MORZENTI A. and PEZZE M. 1988 *On the role of software reliability in software engineering*. In [Bit88], pp 43-67.

[GoG75]    GOODENOUGH J.B. and GERHART S.L 1975 'Toward a theory of test data selection' *SIGPLAN Not.*, **10**(6) pp 493-510.

[Gil70]    GILDERSLEEVE T.R. 1970 *Decision Tables and Their Practical Application in Data Processing*, Prentice Hall.

[Han89]    HANDY C. 1989 *The Age of Unreason*. Business Books Ltd. (ISBN 0091740886).

[HaP88]    HATLEY D.J. and PIRBHAI I.A. 1988 *Strategies for real-time system specification*. Dorset House Publishing.

[Jac75]    JACKSON M.A. 1975 *Principles of Program Design* Academic Press.

[KeP74]    KERNIGHAN B. and PLAUGER P. 1974 *The Elements of Programming Style*. McGraw-Hill.

[KiP85]    KING M.J. and PARDOE J.P. 1985 *Program Design Using JSP - a Practical Introduction*. Macmillan.

[Las89]    LASKI J. 1989 'Testing in the program development cycle'. *Soft.Eng.J.* **4**(2) pp 95-106.

[Lev87]    LEVY L.S. 1987 *Taming the tiger: software engineering and software economics*. Springer.

[Lip72]    LIPOW M. 1972 *Estimation of software package residual errors*. TWR software series report SS-72-09.

[Mil56]    MILLER G. 1956 *The Magical Number Seven Plus or Minus Two: Some Limits on Our Capacity for Processing Information.* Physchological Review, Vol 63 (1956) pp. 81-97.

[Mye75]    MYERS G J *1975 Reliable Software Through Composite Design.* Van Nostrand Reinhold.

[Mye78]    MYERS G.J. 1978 *A controlled experiment in program testing and code walkthroughs/inspections.* Communications of the ACM **21**(9) pp 760-8.

[Mye79]    MYERS G.J. 1979 *The Art of Software Testing.* Wiley.

[Oul90]    OULD M. (*ed.*) 1990 *A standard for software module testing (issue 0.3, 3rd January 1990). Praxis plc: usenet* mao@praxis.co.uk, for the Software Testing Working Group.

[Per77]    PERRIENS M.P. 1977 *An application of formal inspections to top-down structured program development.* RADC-TR-77-212, IBM Federal Systems Division, Gaithersburg, MD (NTIS AD/A-041645).

[Pre87]    PRESSMAN R.S. 1987 *Software engineering, a practitioner's approach (2nd edition).* McGraw-Hill International.

[Rat87]    RATCLIFF B. 1987 *Software Engineering: Principles and Methods.* Blackwell Scientific Publications

[Som85]    SOMMERVILLE I. 1985 *Software engineering (2nd edition).* Addison-Wesley International.

[TeH77]    TEICHROW D. and HERSHEY E.A. III 1977 *PSL/PSA: A computer-aided technique for structured documentation and analysis of information processing systems.* IEEE Tran.S.E. **SE-3** pp 41-8.

[TLN78]    THAYER R.A., LIPOW M. and NELSON E.C. 1978 *Software reliability.* North-Holland.

[Tof70]    TOFFLER A. 1970 *Future Shock.* Pan. (ISBN 0330028618)

[War74]    WARNIER J.D. 1974 *Logical Construction of Programs.* Van Nostrand Reinhold.

[Wei71]    WEINBERG G. 1971 *The psychology of computer programming.* Van Nostrand Reinhold.

[YoC79]    YOURDON E. & CONSTANTINE L. 1979 *Structured Design.* Prentice Hall

[You82]    YOURDON E. 1982 *Managing the system life cycle.* Yourdon Press.

# Index

# About the authors

**Mike Stannett** is *Lecturer in Software Systems Engineering* and head of the *Formal Methods Research Group* in the Department of Computer Science at Sheffield University. Having obtained his Phd in Mathematics in 1986, he went on to study business administration, on the one hand, and formal specification techniques on the other. He is a co-investigator on the prestigious DTI/IED *Silicon towards 2000* project, developing functional test-set generation techniques for high-integrity VLSI.

**Sean Dickinson** is a software engineer with experience of analysis, design and implementation of systems, mainly in banking and healthcare. He is a graduate in computer science.


The authors may be contacted c/o Dept of Computer Science, The University, Sheffield, S10 2TN, UK.

**Janet: AC1MPS@uk.ac.shefpa**

## GENERAL COMPUTING BOOKS

**Compiler Physiology for Beginners,** M Farmer, 279pp, ISBN 0-86238-064-2
**Dictionary of Computer and Information Technology,** D Lynch, 225 pages,
ISBN 0-86238-128-2
**File Structure and Design,** M Cunningham, 211pp, ISBN 0-86238-065-0
**Information Technology Dictionary of Acronyms and Abbreviations,** D Lynch,
270pp, ISBN 0-86238-153-3
**The IBM Personal Computer with BASIC and PC-DOS,** B Kynning, 320pp,
ISBN 0-86238-080-4
**Project Skills Handbook,** S Rogerson, 143pp, ISBN 0-86238-146-0

## PROGRAMMING LANGUAGES

**An Intro to LISP,** P Smith, 130pp, ISBN 0-86238-187-8
**An Intro to OCCAM 2 Programming: 2nd Ed,** Bowler, *et al,* 109pp,
ISBN 0-86238-227-0
**C Simply,** M Parr, 168pp, ISBN 0-86238-262-9
**Cobol for Mainframe and Micro: 2nd Ed,** D Watson, 177pp, ISBN 0-86238-211-4
**Comparative Languages: 2nd Ed,** J R Malone, 125pp, ISBN 0-86238-123-1
**Fortran 77 for Non-Scientists,** P Adman, 109pp, ISBN 0-86238-074-X
**Fortran 77 Solutions to Non-Scientific Problems,** P Adman, 150pp,
ISBN 0-86238-087-1
**Fortran Lectures at Oxford,** F Pettit, 135pp, ISBN 0-86238-122-3
**LISP: From Foundations to Applications,** G Doukidis *et al,* 228pp,
ISBN 0-86238-191-6
**Programming for Change in Pascal,** D Robson, 272pp, ISBN 0-86238-250-5
**Prolog versus You,** A Johansson, *et al,* 308pp, ISBN 0-86238-174-6
**Simula Begin,** G M Birtwistle, *et al,* 391pp, ISBN 0-86238-009-X
**Structured Programming with COBOL & JSP: Vol 1,** J B Thompson, 372pp,
ISBN 0-86238-154-1, **Vol 2,** 354pp, ISBN 0-86238-245-9
**The Intensive C Course: 2nd Edition,** M Farmer, 186pp, ISBN 0-86238-190-8
**The Intensive Pascal Course: 2nd Edition,** M Farmer, 125pp, ISBN 0-86238-219-X

## ASSEMBLY LANGUAGE PROGRAMMING

**Coding the 68000,** N Hellawell, 214pp, ISBN 0-86238-180-0
**Computer Organisation and Assembly Language Programming,** L Ohlsson & P
Stenstrom, 128pp, ISBN 0-86238-129-0
**What is machine code and what can you do with it?** N Hellawell, 104pp,
ISBN 0-86238-132-0

## PROGRAMMING TECHNIQUES

**Discrete-events simulations models in PASCAL/MT+ on a microcomputer,** L P
Jennergren, 135pp, ISBN 0-86238-053-7
**Information and Coding,** J A Llewellyn, 152pp, ISBN 0-86238-099-5
**JSP - A Practical Method of Program Design,** L Ingevaldsson, 204pp,
ISBN 0-86238-107-X
**Modular Software Design,** M Stannett, 136pp, ISBN 0-86238-266-1

**Linear Programming: A Computational Approach: 2nd Ed,** K K Lau, 150pp,
ISBN 0-86238-182-7
**Programming for Beginners: the structured way,** D Bell & P Scott, 178pp,
ISBN 0-86238-130-4
**Software Engineering for Students,** M Coleman & S Pratt, 195pp,
ISBN 0-86238-115-0
**Software Taming with Dimensional Design,** M Coleman & S Pratt, 164pp,
ISBN 0-86238-142-8
**Systems Programming with JSP,** B Sanden, 186pp, ISBN 0-86238-054-5

## MATHEMATICS AND COMPUTING
**Fourier Transforms in Action,** F Pettit, 133pp, ISBN 0-86238-088-X
**Generalised Coordinates,** L G Chambers, 90pp, ISBN 0-86238-079-0
**Statistics and Operations Research,** I P Schagen, 300pp, ISBN 0-86238-077-4
**Teaching of Modern Engineering Mathematics,** L Rade (ed), 225pp,
ISBN 0-86238-173-8
**Teaching of Statistics in the Computer Age,** L Rade (ed), 248pp, ISBN 0-86238-090-1
**The Essentials of Numerical Computation,** M Bartholomew-Biggs, 241pp,
ISBN 0-86238-029-4

## DATABASES AND MODELLING
**Computer Systems Modelling & Development,** D Cornwell, 291pp,
ISBN 0-86238-220-3
**An Introduction to Data Structures,** B Boffey, D Yates, 250pp, ISBN 0-86238-076-6
**Database Analysis and Design: 2nd Ed,** H Robinson, 378pp, ISBN 0-86238-018-9
**Databases and Database Systems: 2nd Ed,** E Oxborrow, 256pp, ISBN 0-86238-091-X
**Data Bases and Data Models,** B Sundgren, 134pp, ISBN 0-86238-031-6
**Text Retrieval and Document Databases,** J Ashford & P Willett, 125pp,
ISBN 0-86238-204-1
**Information Modelling,** J Bubenko (ed), 687pp, ISBN 0-86238-006-5

## UNIX
**An Intro to the Unix Operating System,** C Duffy, 152pp, ISBN 0-86238-143-6
**Operating Systems through Unix,** G Emery, 96pp, ISBN 0-86238-086-3

## SYSTEMS ANALYSIS & SYSTEMS DESIGN
**Systems Analysis and Development: 3rd Ed,** P Layzell & P Loucopoulos, 284pp,
ISBN 0-86238-215-7
**SSADM Techniques,** Lejk, et al, 350pp, ISBN 0-86238-224-6
**Computer Systems: Where Hardware meets Software,** C Machin, 200pp,
ISBN 0-86238-075-8
**Microcomputer Systems: hardware and software,** J Tierney, 168pp,
ISBN 0-86238-218-1
**Distributed Applications and Online Dialogues: a design method for application
systems,** A Rasmussen, 271pp, ISBN 0-86238-105-3

# HARDWARE

**Computers from First Principles,** M Brown, 128pp, ISBN 0-86238-027-8
**Fundamentals of Microprocessor Systems,** P Witting, 525pp, ISBN 0-86238-030-8

# ELECTRICAL & ELECTRONIC ENGINEERING

**Analogue & Digital Signal Processing & Coding,** P Grant, 450pp,
ISBN 0-86238-206-8
**Handbook of Electronics,** J de Sousa Pires, approx 750pp, ISBN 0-86238-061-8
**Electricity,** T Johansson, 960pp, ISBN 0-86238-208-4
**Interference-free Electronics,** S Benda, ISBN 0-86238-255-6

# NETWORKS

**Communication Network Protocols: 2nd Ed,** B Marsden, 345pp,
ISBN 0-86238-106-1
**Computer Networks: Fundamentals and Practice,** M D Bacon *et al,* 109pp,
ISBN 0-86238-028-6
**Data Networks 1,** Ericsson & Televerket, 250pp, ISBN 0-86238-193-2
**Data Networks 2,** Ericsson & Televerket, 159pp, ISBN 0-86238-221-1
**Telecommunications: Telephone Networks 1,** Ericsson & Televerket, 147pp,
ISBN 0-86238-093-6
**Telecommunications: Telephone Networks 2,** Ericsson & Televerket, 176pp,
ISBN 0-86238-113-4

# GRAPHICS

**An Introductory Course in Computer Graphics,** R Kingslake, 146pp,
ISBN 0-86238-073-1
**Techniques of Interactive Computer Graphics,** A Boyd, 242pp, ISBN 0-86238-024-3
**Two-dimensional Computer Graphics,** S Laflin, 85pp, ISBN 0-86238-127-4

# APPLICATIONS

**Computers in Health and Fitness,** J Abas, 106pp, ISBN 0-86238-155-X
**Developing Expert Systems,** G Doukidis, E Whitley, ISBN 0-86238-196-7
**Expert Systems Introduced,** D Daly, 180pp, ISBN 0-86238-185-1
**Handbook of Finite Element Software,** J Mackerle & B Fredriksson, approx
1000pp, ISBN 0-86238-135-5
*Inside* **Data Processing: computers and their effective use in business: 2nd Ed,**
A deWatteville, 150pp, ISBN 0-86238-252-1
**Modelling with Spreadsheets,** A Rothery, 200pp, ISBN 0-86238-258-0
**Proceedings of the Third Scandinavian Conference on Image Analysis,** P
Johansen & P Becker (eds) 426pp, ISBN 0-86238-039-1
**Programmable Control Systems,** G Johannesson, 136pp, ISBN 0-86238-046-4
**Risk and Reliability Appraisal on Microcomputers,** G Singh, with G Kiangi,
142pp, ISBN 0-86238-159-2
**Statistics with Lotus 1-2-3: 2nd Ed,** M Lee & J Soper, 207pp, ISBN 0-86238-244-0

## HCI

**Human/Computer Interaction: from voltage to knowledge,** J Kirakowski, 250pp, ISBN 0-86238-179-7
**Information Ergonomics,** T Ivegard, 228pp, ISBN 0-86238-032-4
**Computer Display Designer's Handbook,** E Wagner, approx 300pp, ISBN 0-86238-171-1

## INFORMATION AND SOCIETY

**Access to Government Records: International Perspectives and Trends,** T Riley, 112pp, ISBN 0-86238-119-3
**CAL/CBT - the great debate,** D Marshall, 300pp, ISBN 0-86238-144-4
**Economic and Trade-Related Aspects of Transborder Dataflow,** R Wellington-Brown, 93pp, ISBN 0-86238-110-X
**Information Technology and a New International Order,** J Becker, 141pp, ISBN 0-86238-043-X
**People or Computers: Three Ways of Looking at Information Systems,** M Nurminen, 1218pp, ISBN 0-86238-184-3
**Transnational Data Flows in the Information Age,** C Hamelink, 115pp, ISBN 0-86238-042-1

## SCIENCE HANDBOOKS

**Alpha Maths Handbook,** L Rade, 199pp, ISBN 0-86238-036-7
**Beta Maths Handbook,** L Rade, 425pp, ISBN 0-86238-140-1
**Nuclear Analytical Chemistry,** D Brune *et al,* 557pp, ISBN 0-86238-047-2
**Physics Handbook,** C Nordling & J Osterman, 430pp, ISBN 0-86238-037-5
**The V-Belt Handbook,** H Palmgren, 287pp, ISBN 0-86238-111-8

Chartwell-Bratt specialise in excellent books at affordable prices.

For further details contact your local bookshop, or ring Chartwell-Bratt direct on **081-467 1956** (Access/Visa welcome.)

Ring or write for our *free* catalogue.

**Chartwell-Bratt (Publishing & Training) Ltd,** Old Orchard, Bickley Road, Bromley, Kent, BR1 2NE, United Kingdom.
Tel 081-467 1956, Fax 081-467 1754